Skipper Swede's

little

Book of Yachting

On this book

The idea for this book came into existence during some horribly boring night watches on a Mediterranean crossing from Gibraltar to Greece in an early spring. To avoid falling asleep during the night shifts, one's brain had the good taste to come up with all kinds of bizarre thought patterns to mercilessly shock the owner of said brain into 'awakeness'. And in this case, it did a pretty good job at it. As a matter of fact, it did such a good job that Skipper Swede decided that this book should be produced in honour of the madness that is the human mind, lost at sea.

Besides, when you've spent several days of not seeing anything other than water, water and some more water, a necessity to entertain oneself emerges and this book is a pleasant little collection of those humoristic moments. However, since you are so starved for just the tiniest of a laugh, you would literally think that the cries of the seagulls, a penis-shaped cloud, or a loud reverberating fart in your own cabin is the most amazing contribution to comedy in recent history. So my dear reader, don't get your hopes up.

This book will at times present you with a less than fine use of the English language. This is partly because Skipper Swede is in fact Swedish and therefore from a country where English is not the first language. It vould be qutie apresiated if you kut Skipper Swede som slaq in dis matteuer.

The other, more dominant reason to inadequate and sometimes foul language in this book, is simply because Skipper Swede is a sailor and, as we all know, sailors swear. Ferociously. Permanently. And with a passion. You will not find any salty sea-dogs on the world's oceans who doesn't swear like, as it were, a sailor. However, for the respect of both storytelling in itself and for my respect for you as the reader, I've tried to tone it the fuck down throughout the book.

We all know that life at sea provides you with amazing experiences and intriguing stories to be retold. Naturally, this book provides a collection of this as well, and you will find plenty of real-life situations described here. Skipper Swede has included his own observations of what is transpiring in the yachting world, along with his most personal and sincere opinions of both people, places and happenings. However, just because Skipper Swede is quite opinionated doesn't mean that he's just not in fact taking the piss. Things you are about to read are there just to be a bit provoking, entertaining and a bit of fun. Don't take it too seriously.

And with that said, the classic Hollywood-based disclaimer is repeated here as well: *All characters appearing in this work are fictitious. Any resemblance to real persons, living or dead, is purely coincidental.* This is obviously not true at all, since no-one could have such a vivid imagination to come up with all this crazy stuff. So the stories are indeed true and have been experienced by Skipper Swede, but names, locations and time has been altered to the point where they are no longer recognizable to the actual events. It's basically Skipper Swede's get-out-of-jail card, which can prove useful in case some idiot feels that the author is Riverdancing on some teeny-weeny toes throughout the book. Besides, if you are the kind of jerk to feel offended and think that you are the protagonist in Skipper Swede's rant, you might want to contemplate what kind of stupid shit you did to end up there in the first place.

That's the kind of book you are about to read. Exciting, isn't it!

So in essence, this is the foreword, explaining what you can expect from this book. And let me be formidably clear and point out that there's no real structure in the assembly of pages you are holding in your hands, there's no order between the chapters or the stories and it's just a collection of things that you might, or might not, encounter in the Yachting world. In other words, this book is just a fine study in Skipper Swede's mentally imbalanced rambling.

And keeping to the tradition of stories from the sea, every single fish in this book was THIS big.

Since this is the foreword, Skipper Swede would also like to take this opportunity to thank all the amazing contributors to this book. Without the knowledgeable, interesting and heart-warming people, along with all the other nitwits and blockheads I've met, this book would not be as substantial as it is, nor would it contain the quite remarkable, outlandish and absurd stories your are about to read.

Some of this stuff is frankly so far-out that it would be a crime against mankind not to reiterate the asinine events that has occurred and let the world enjoy the silliness of them.

So to sum up this little introduction, I sincerely hope that you will enjoy this book. It has indeed been a journey writing it, worthy of any ocean crossing or worldwide circumnavigation. Composing this work has been an amazing experience, a hilarious undertaking, and I really wish that you will have as many laughs while diving into it, if not more, as I've had during the creation of this very questionable masterpiece.

Enjoy my little book of yachting. Keep laughing! Keep sailing!

Skipper Swede

Index:

See next page

With what has just been explained,
then why, by Poseidon's *fork*, would you need an index
for a book like this?

Read this book any bloody way
you please.

Rules of Sailing

Critical guidelines to live by while at sea

Rule no 1.
Look cool.

Rule no 2.
If shit is about to happen,
has already happened,
or is to everyone's amusement presently happening,
see Rule 1.

Rule no 3.
Skip is always right.
Therefore Rule 1 applies constantly
and automatically.

On Yachting

As the observant reader would notice, this chapter contains the same word as the title of the book itself. And if Skipper Swede would be a cheeky bastard, he would without any hesitation make this the only chapter of the book and thereby saving himself a lot of time and effort in writing this whole god damn thing.

Go directly to 'GO' and collect 200 dollars, as it were.

However, Skipper Swede is in fact quite a nice guy, to the contrary of what various rumours imply, so you, my dear reader, will be able to enjoy plenty of more embellished stories, crappy jokes and questionable entertainment in the following pages. Besides, if there would be just one chapter in this book, it would be quite possible that you would be a bit disappointed and would rather see Skipper Swede Go To Jail. And not just that, but to Go *Directly* To Jail. Do not pass GO, do not collect 200 dollars.

So although this whole book is Skipper Swede's personal reflection of Yachting, there are some things that needs to be addressed about this topic in general and that is exactly what we will do in this chapter. And the first business on the agenda is "Why, for the love of everything that is holy, do we enjoy yachting in the first place?"

I implore you, dear reader, to think about it. Regardless if you are a seasoned sailor with thousands of miles under your belt, an ostrich cruiser that pops out when it seems convenient, or a fully-fledged landlubber whose closest encounter with boats is when you play with one in the bathtub, the question still remains. When scrutinized logically, it becomes obvious that the whole ordeal is an intricate study in human mental illness. "Why?" you might ask, and the answer is simple. If you are not nutty as a fruitcake, why else would you bob around on the water in a tiny container made of wood, plastic or metal? Or ferro-cement, which is almost a stone. Stones do not float, last time I checked. Neither does metal nor most plastic. And considering the plates, rigging, keel and other bits of steel, aluminium and lead in a wooden boat, it is safe to assume that a wooden vessel will also aspire, with great eagerness, to become a submarine whenever opportunity presents itself. And we venture out with great zest in one of these suicide-coffins? Into an environment that is more than often quite unpredictable, quite dramatic and quite angry? In an element where we can't breathe and if we would try our life is gone faster than a toupée in a hurricane?

No, I'm telling you that it's madness. If it wasn't for all the psychologists who enjoy sailing as well, the whole yachting community would probably have been given nice, white, long-sleeved jackets and accommodation in a comfortably padded room a long time ago.

Some of these oddballs argue that sailing brings you close to nature, that you are in touch with the elements, that there is bliss and serenity at sea and all kinds of other new-age nonsense. I have to agree wholeheartedly with all of it. It does indeed bring you closer to nature. Sometimes it almost merges you with nature. One especially realises this when the freezing air manages to find its way through your supposedly wind-proof weather gear and drop your body temperature with at least 10 degrees. Then you really feel that you are one with the wilderness. And you are certainly in touch with the elements as your clothes are permanently soaked and attaches to your body like wet, rancid cheese from Denmark. Not to forget the caress of nature when you receive a loving embrace from the ocean in the form of a supersonic projectile of sea-spray. Often into your face when you least expect it. You have to admit that one cannot find a better lover than the ocean.

It is said that sailing can be defined as *'The fine art of standing fully clothed in a cold shower, while examining your last meal and tearing up $100 bills'*. But somehow that does not sound particularly exciting to me. I already know what I had for supper. After all, I was the one eating it. I sincerely doubt that I will make any breakthroughs by revisiting that particular experience in reverse. And I certainly won't win the Nobel Prize in economics for relieving the world from a few notes of currency.

So perhaps this exhibition in human stupidity boils down to history? After all, the saying 'Navigare Necesse Est' is said to speak for itself. That it is necessary to be out on the water, with all what that implies. And perhaps it is, when we look at the days of old in seafaring. To venture out in the unknown, to discover new and uncharted territories. To explore. That would indeed justify the suffering we put ourselves through by being out there. Without standing up to the challenges of months and years at sea, in horrendous conditions and in risk of one's very life, we would not have reached the far corners of the earth. And the merchant navy falls close to that category of seafaring as well, as we would never have sampled the riches of those far corners, unless vessels had crossed oceans. Even in this day and age when most of the globe has been explored, the merchant navy still fulfils an extremely important role and many modern conveniences would not be available, should the ships stay in port. So perhaps seafaring is justified in the situations when it's professional in nature. But then why are the salaries so embarrassingly low and most workers so bloody underpaid? Anyone care to explain?

And whilst on that subject, not only do mariners get paid peanuts for the work they do, everything in this industry is also horrendously overpriced. The mark-up is distressfully comical, and you can only head in to the nearest chandlery to see that a nut or bolt you buy in the hardware store for a few pennies will cost a few pounds in the marine outlet, just because some greedy moron has put a tag on it that says: 'For Boats'.

So you don't get paid enough if you do it professionally, you gladly fork out gargantuan expenses if you do it as a hobby, and all to be able to head out on a very questionable adventure where you get freezing cold, soaking wet, and generally uncomfortable no matter where you try to sit. Well out there, you are in effect not really going anywhere, and you are doing so quite slowly. And when you get back in (if you get back in) you get to hang out with your sailing buddies, which quite frankly is just a bunch of self-absorbed twats that will gladly explain to you in detail what you did wrong on your trip and what they would have done much better than you. When they are finally done with their rant, you get treated to hours on hours of reiteration of how much more fascinating endeavours at sea they've had.

When put into that perspective it becomes evident that yachting doesn't hold any water, so to speak. Frankly, anyone who thinks that yachting is the logical choice to pursue could probably not pour water from a boot even if the instructions were on the heel. Yachting is just pure asininity, an exercise in lunacy, done by people paddling a canoe with only one oar. So to revisit my original question: Why do we love it so much?

Let me tell you why.

We do it because it's the coolest thing in the world. We do it because there is nothing more awesome in the entire universe. There is no other activity so ultimately challenging and daring than all the various forms of sailing. There is also no other activity that can be as enormously rewarding. It is namely by struggling through all those previously mentioned ordeals that you feel a sense of achievement. It is by testing your endurance and pushing yourself to the limits that makes you evolve. And when you've fought through all those trials that yachting consists of, and you have succeeded, the level of gratification is unrivalled.

Yachting will test your endurance. It separates the wheat from the chaff. Heading out around the Horn, taking a trip through the North Sea, or cruising down to Hobart are not necessarily a display in foolishness as much as it is a benchmark of capabilities. Racing single-handedly around the worlds fiercest oceans is a statement of independence and spirit. Pushing yourself for days in conditions unworthy of human habitat proves that everything else in life is a walk in the park. And all the other hardships sailors endure with ease put us right up there with Chuck Norris.

Just think about what we talked about earlier in this chapter and you will see that yachting is the raw material for building superheroes. Everything goes against it; against succeeding, against pleasure, even against surviving, and yet we overcome. We don't care about the cold, the wetness, the wind or the uncomfortable. We're too hard-nosed to even notice and would rather just make a mental note to get better waterproofs next time out. We don't care about being constantly ill, the negative money situation or even social differences on board. We are uncompromising enough to focus on what matters, namely perseverance. A yacht can sink and you can drown, and you're hard-boiled enough to know this and get on with the job without flinching. No other lifestyle breeds such hard-core people that could survive for months eating their own socks and who can find comfortable sleeping arrangements in a washing-machine. Yachting is a birthplace for genuine rock stars and that is also why sailors are the coolest people in the world. We have no fear. We're not pussy-footing around. We just get out there and do our thing.

So the reason why we love yachting is because it's the coolest, most insane and most challenging thing to do. You're either mad as a hatter or a right flippin' die-hard to be a sailor. Probably both. And that is why you get to belong to the most stiff-necked, gung-ho, radical and awesome crowd in the world.

Not only do we look cool. We are cool!

EAT   SLEEP   SAIL   LOOK
                                  COOL

Nautical terms, lesson 1

Leeward
The most natural direction for paper charts to travel towards before disappearing.

Windward
The most disgusting direction to be seasick.

Overboard
A natural eco-storage for cell phones, wallets, cutlery, tools, crew and other important affects.

A quick comparison

If you are not already a sailor, then I know what you are thinking. You think that we are delusional. You think that sailing is about bobbing around under a sunny sky in a tropical paradise sipping on cocktails. I can well appreciate that false assumption, and that's why I've compiled a list of comparison between yachting and other activities to clear you of your hallucinations.

Activities, sports, lifestyles and jobs. No particular order:

• Skydiving is a dare-devil sport. Jumping out of a plane at 12'500ft. Air whizzing past you as ground approaches fast. Crazy stuff, right? Wrong. Try operating a chunk of 15+ tonnes through a spray-infused storm between 20ft brick walls of water that constantly try to collapse on top of you and sometimes succeeds. Whilst you enjoy a hot cup of tea. That is crazy stuff.

• Motorcross. Evil Knievel and the likes. Whether on a track, through terrain, jumping boulders or doing trial, these madcaps risk serious injury or even death by their stunts. Is it wicked? Sure, but not in comparison to manhandling 500 square meters of sail holding 3000 tonnes of load, maintaining your balance on a slippery surface that moves around like a 3 dimensional piston, while hoping not to get perforated by sharp objects or have your head taken off by stuff or crewmembers flying around. To say that sailing is wicked is an understatement. But to us it's just another day at work.

• Snowboarding. Same as with skiing, a sport that utilizes water in its still, solid and frozen form. That's cool. So imagine if you were snowboarding down a very steep mountain, in a blizzard, over an avalanche, whilst the mountain surface is bubbling like a Jacuzzi. And your board is 60 feet long and constantly on the verge of doing the complete opposite of what you want. Then you could start imagining what sailing is like.

• Parkour and free running. Urban stuntmen traversing rooftops and performing breath-taking acrobatics. A true test of endurance and physical action? Not really. Imagine getting airborne, thrown around and defying the laws of gravity at the same time as you are lifting more weights than you would pull in the gym, while running a 100 meter track full speed taking a shit. Wearing a dry suit. That's action. Really unpleasant action.

• Extreme canoeing. Riding in a specially designed craft with only a double ended paddle for both propulsion and steerage. Racing down dangerous white-water rapids, dodging rocks and waterfalls. Yeah. Try doing that using only the wind for momentum, in a thunderstorm, going up the falls instead of down, and you're doing what we do before breakfast.

• Formula One racing. Now that's badass. You get to sit comfortably in a vehicle with suspension and drive around on the same smooth track for hours. There are no obstacles, only other competitors that you have to avoid. And you need to manage your speed in the curves not to slide off the road. Every now and then you can easily replace worn-down items on your car by cruising in to the pit-stop. For sailors, that's easier than a spin around the harbour in calm weather.

• Back packing. World travelling. To challenge yourself during a lengthy period of time, meeting dodgy characters, getting little or no sleep in hostels, sampling strange local food and living on a shoe-string budget. What an adventurous life experience! Not really. Unless you do all of that while hanging out with sailors 24-7, sleeping on a constantly wet bunk in clothes that never dries and smells like rotten vegetables, fuelling yourself with nothing but freeze-dried goo and experiencing violent diarrhoea on an equally violently pendular toilet, then you could claim to have the adventure of a lifetime. Oh, and shoestring budget? What's the challenge in having a budget in the first place?!

• Fighter pilots. The Top Guns. Awesome guys who sings 'Great Balls of Fire' and play muscle-flex -volleyball on the beach in their spare time. At work they endure serious G-forces, engage in dramatic dog-fights and display superior tactical prowess. A bunch of amateurs. If they would sing some good tunes and stop flexing to impress the other faggots, they might stand a chance to be allowed to scrub the decks on a yacht. But they will never be allowed to come near the Nav-station on a boat nor engage in the tactical decisions of a match-race. Because on a boat you can't just throw in the towel and do what all fighter pilots have been taught to do when they are facing imminent danger. On a boat, there is no label that says 'Eject'. If there was a label, it would say 'Suck it up, Bitch'.

• Astronauts. Probably one of the most similar professions to hard-core yachting. Extremely hard physical preparation, extensive knowledge and problem-solving abilities, live in cramped quarters, spend lengthy times in solitude, eat nasty food and re-evaluate your toilet routines. Risk of suffocation and death is noticeable and always present. But you get to be weightless in space. Only time a sailor is weightless is when the vessel interrupts its journey by nose-diving at 20-plus knots, resulting in a pitch-pole catapulting the crew into oblivion. Perhaps if you combine a fighter pilot and an astronaut and you have a sailor. Oh, and add extreme watersports to it. And professional weightlifting. And rugby during a weather-related apocalypse. You know what? Just forget it.

I could continue with other so-called extreme sports, activities and lifestyles, such as Ice Climbing and Rock Climbing (seriously, you're going up a flat wall), Mountaineering (afternoon stroll up a hill with possibility for overnight stay under the stars), Mountainbiking (riding down the hill to buy some groceries), Skateboarding (doing fancy tricks on a solid wave of plywood), Paintball (running around playing war and spraying colours on each other), Paragliding and Hang-gliding (checking out your house from above), Rugby (running after a poorly designed ball and cuddling with other men in the process), American Football (the pussy-version of rugby) and so on. However, with these examples I hope that you have been enlightened adequately to understand the superiority of sailing. And as you can see with these comparisons, sailing is the most awesome thing in the world, and sailors are the coolest breed there is. If you are not already engaged in yachting, then drop your shit and start sailing!

Nautical terms, lesson 2

Ahoy
The FIRST in the collection of four letter words that sailors greet each other with. Others begin with 'C', 'D' and 'F'. You do the math.

Accidental gybe
An occurrence where the crew performs amazing movements to avoid getting slung off the boat. Later developed into an American dance form.

Hatch
An opening on deck which allows for premature and ungraceful arrival into any random cabin.

On Sailors and yachting characters

So, there should now be no questions about the unchallenged awesomeness of yachting. It is something that everyone should aspire to do, and something that produces the coolest people in the world.

At least that's what sailors themselves tend to think. We'll get to that in a moment.

The previous hubris-infused explanation of yachting aside, it's worth mentioning that yachting can indeed be a fantastic enterprise providing lots of great experiences for its participants. Regardless if you get involved in cruising, racing or do it as your profession, you are guaranteed to have an active and interesting lifestyle that gives you an abundance of memories, friends and stories to tell. The yachting community itself is something wonderful to be part of, and as you walk into the yacht club you are instantly greeted to the point where you can almost hear people loudly cheering "Norm!" at your entrance. The sailing community is also characterised by remarkable assistance and support, to a level bordering on true altruism. The sense of community and desire to help each other out is often so remarkably benevolent that it makes even the toughest sailor a bit misty-eyed.

Just after I had purchased my boat in the Caribbean, I was constantly approached by fellow sailors that offered their help and suggestions. I got information on everything from people's knowledge and expertise in repair work and fiberglassing, to actual hands-on assistance in gel-coating and rigging refitting. Within half a year I had acquired a VHF-radio, a cockpit tent, an outboard, an auto-pilot, an anchor and an abundance of other things that people handed down to me. And most of them were insulted when I asked to pay for either the items or their work. Likewise, when one of the hurricanes had devastated that particular island and left vessels destroyed, homes ripped apart and dreams annihilated, the fundraising and social conscience during the aftermath was on the level with any world-wide humanitarian charity organisation.

Thanks to the immense level of experiences that yachting provides, it is no surprise that sailors always have a fascinating story to tell. And even though they fall dangerously close to fishermen's stories, one shouldn't be surprised if most are both reasonably true and first-person experiences. I have yet to come across a sailor who doesn't have a story to tell, and an honourable mention is a friend and former instructor of mine called Phil. He told fantastic stories of various episodes of his sailing life and not only did they prove valid points in his teaching, they also served as funny illustrations and entertainment during the courses. Every single story of his started off on quite a happy upbeat, with the protagonist succeeding in his undertakings, and slowly transformed into a complete disaster of epic proportions. His stories would always end with shipwrecking, hospitalisation, capsizing, sinking of the vessel or any other fiasco of your choice. And it all reflected quite aptly how it can be out there on the water, and how quickly a situation can turn to hair, teeth, eyes and brain all over the place.

Since we were an optimistic bunch, we promptly named our instructor 'Lucky Phil'. Always look on the bright side of life, so to speak.

So because of all the things that yachting provides, it is no wonder that sailors are a bunch of characters. Yachting in itself with its majestic experiences, unparalleled philosophy and trialling tests of endurance will instantly transform its participants. Not only do they come from all walks of life and have all kinds of backgrounds, but you will find everything from hippies and the marine equivalent of tree-hugging bohemians, to down-to-earth and hands-on engineers and physicists. The variety of people you'll get to meet is staggering, and the individuals themselves are pleasantly crazy in their own right. Sailors are undoubtedly a bit weird, most often in a delightfully charming and sympathetic way.

If you haven't yet experienced this wonderful diversity of pronounced characters, then head down to your nearest yacht club or take a stroll around your local marina. You are guaranteed to have an invigorating experience including anything from graceful swan dives from sterns into the murky harbour water, to choice of clothing that would make David Bowie look like an amateur. Try keeping a straight face when talking to someone wearing a 3000£ Musto Ocean foul weather gear outfit, and a pair of yellow Crocs.

So yachting does indeed foster some delightful characters and individuals with unique and amusing quirks. But as with any coin there is a flipside to this as well, and this particular sandwich has an impressive ability to land butter-side down.

See, it's virtually impossible to be involved in something as awesome as yachting, an activity that is said to produce rock stars, superheroes and supposedly the coolest breed in the world, without it also producing an astronomically huge narcissism in its participants. Sailing is an ego-trip without comparison and sailors will naturally believe that they are the centre of any available universe. As agreeable as they might be, it is just an unfortunate and simple fact that sailors are inherently full of themselves. It comes with the hat, so to speak. Or in this case; the Southwester.

Everywhere you go, you will find sailors who will claim to have done more than you and experienced more than you. They will argue that they have more knowledge than you and that they are right in every respect. In other words, they are in their own opinion, The Shit. Especially in comparison to you. It is undoubtedly difficult to be so cool, and not also be a complete and utter twat.

One thing that gets old really fast is that sailors always have a better story to tell. They've already experienced something much more fantastic than you, and their endeavours are far more interesting than yours. They are the heroes in their own version of Lord of the Rings and they display a manic need to tell the world about it. And they happily do so for the same amount of time that it took Peter Jackson to tell his version, bonus-scenes, extra material and all. *How about you shut it and listen to someone else for a change?*

But because they have experienced something much more fantastic and interesting than anyone else, they falsely assume that they must also be right in everything. Therefore their opinion is per definition correct and needs to be brutally announced for the benefit of the poor half-wits present. So a lot of sailors have an opinion. About pretty much everything. This can, and will, become mortally infuriating as you will be constantly interrupted by someone who is on a mission to express his own grandeur. Take any conversation you would like to have with a person and ruin it after your first sentence, or possibly half-way through, and you will have how it can be to talk to a stuck-up-their-own-arse sailor.

As you read through the following replies, put some emphasis on the words 'I', 'me' and 'my' and say them about five times as slow and three times as loud as the rest of the sentence. They are after all the most important words in the sailors head.

"So I went to have a coffee at 'John's' place today (and I'm about to tell you what happened)."
"Let ME tell you that I don't like that place, I think the coffee is awful. I always drink MY coffee at 'Oceans'. That's where I have MY best coffee. They really know how to make it there. Blablabla ad infinitum."

"So, I watched the new movie 'Vengeance' yesterday (and would like to share my experience with you)."
"No, I think it sounds awful. I watched 'Battlefield Earth' yesterday and that's a movie! Have you seen it? I think it's one of the best I've ever seen. Blablabla ad infinitum."

"I'm not sure how I should repair the engine (but I'd like to discuss a few ideas)."
"The first thing you need to do is to listen to ME because I have been on hundreds of boats and I know MY way around engines. There was this one time in the Bay of Biscay where I... blablabla ad infinitum."

"So we should probably leave harbour at 1400 to make the tidal window (and I would like a constructive conversation about it)."
"I have looked at MY Navionics on MY tablet and that says that we can leave at 1800. MY instructor has sailed around the world using only his phone, so he must be right. That's MY take on it and I know it works. Blablabla ad infinitum."

How about you put a sock in it you conceited besserwisser. I wasn't asking for your bloody opinion!

Another thing that is an effect of sailors being too full of themselves, is their fully planted delusion of their own competence. Because they have experiences outperforming The Lord himself and because they have the most interesting and valid opinions, they naturally also assume that they are most competent person in the world. Therefore they always know best. Which is obviously complete poppycock.

A situation that exemplifies this and could have gone horribly wrong was when I received some instructions from a fellow skipper. I was about to depart the dock and had limited manoeuvring space in the basin, and as soon as I was clear of the quay a good 20 knots of wind would blow me back on to the row of boats parked there. He insisted persistently on his instructions and asserted me that it was how it was done, that it was the standard practise in the company and that he had done this manoeuvre the same way for over a year. I was quite new to the company and didn't want to come across as a sailor being too full of myself, so against my better judgement I did what he told me to. Needless to say, there was all of a sudden plenty of people rushing about, even more fenders magically appearing from nowhere, and quite a handful of gel-coat removed from the boats in the process.

He failed to mention that he had never done the manoeuvre under those conditions, or with a powerboat for that matter. But it was for sure good fun to see the new guy cock it up.

I once met a sailor who had YachtMaster Ocean and who worked professionally as a skipper in the Caribbean. On the day of his arrival to the marina, this gentleman felt it terribly important to loudly proclaim his superiority in sailing to each and everyone around. However, after just a bit of detective work it turned out that this wanker couldn't even distinguish between a lateral- and a cardinal marker. If you're not a sailor and doesn't know what that means, it is like the road equivalent of mixing up the sign for 'duck-crossing' with the 'Danger: a T-Rex will have you for lunch'.

Falsely believing that you are the most competent person around is never a good thing, and bragging about it is even worse. A young sailor I met in a marina in the UK was constantly challenging the world and universe itself, claiming that he would sail circles around everyone who lived, had lived or will ever live. He was without a doubt the best sailor to be found and should have a boat, country or even planet named after himself. He then proceeded to promptly land a job worthy of his superior skillset working as a deckhand on a megayacht in Antibes. Well done, loser.

Not all sailors are like this, obviously, and I have personally met an enormous amount who didn't display this awkwardly self-indulgent trait. But there is unfortunately a remarkable percentage of sailors who are so immeasurably full of themselves and as a result just talk loads of rubbish that no one really wants to listen to. It is excellently tiresome to hear sailors going on and on about themselves, about their knowledge, about their opinions and about their competence. This is not only an exercise in advanced lobotomy when you are on the water but on land as well, and it's not only for other sailors but for regular people too. But for the sake of this being a book on yachting, my final statement for this chapter will be for the benefit of sailing-related situations:

If you ever come across a sailor who claims to know everything there is to know, then tell the sailor to shove it and make like a shepherd and get the flock off the boat!

On Competence

Rule no 1.
You are never too old, too knowledgeable or too experienced to learn something new.

Rule no 2.
If you ever come across a person, whether it is the Skipper, First Mate, Deckhand, Chef, Host, Engineer, Owner, Charter Land-based Support or Toilet Cleaner, who claims to be old enough to know everything, who claims to be so knowledgeable that he or she knows everything, or who says they have experienced everything there is to experience and therefore also know everything, then immediately jump ship without hesitation!

Rule no 3.
Never become one of those people. See rule 1.

Nautical terms, lesson 3

Boom:

1.   The sound of a thunder clap.

2.   A horizontal part of the rigging, designed for controlling the sail around the axis of the mast.

3.   The sound that said part of the rig makes when it, on its lateral journey across the boat, hits a crewmember.

On Skippers

Being the master of a vessel requires a lot of knowledge and experience, and it comes with quite a responsibility. As a skipper, you are the one who has legal liability for the vessel and her crew, and the one who has to answer in a court of law when something goes tits up. You have the ultimate say in dealings and decisions on the vessel, since you are the one to face the music when the Eurovision Song Contest starts playing and you really don't fancy to listen to ABBA one more time. The hierarchy on a vessel is not under any circumstance a democracy, but rather a pleasant display in dictatorship. It works, it works well, and it has worked well for centuries.

Unfortunately, this splendidly well-working system also feeds the already ego-infused mind of the sailor with the same efficiency as an American all-you-can-eat buffet in a fat-camp. As the sailor has now been promoted to Skipper, there is no chance in hell that his or her opinions are not more important than the one of God Almighty, that the stories are not outweighing those of Homeros and that he or she is more competent at everything in life than Tony Stark. A skipper is the ultimate anthropomorphic personification of the art of being full of yourself. On the pinnacle of the mountain of self-importance the skipper stand, proud and tall, looking down on the unworthy mortals. Actually, the skipper is not looking down. The skipper is looking horizontally, into a mirror. Whilst pompously masturbating.

By the way, Skipper Swede is certainly no exception. *Fap-fap-fap.*

This is the impression that we skippers give others quite regularly, and some skippers more often than others. If you, my dear reader, have even the slightest interest or experience in sailing, which you probably do as you are reading this book, you will most likely have just as many horror stories to tell about skippers as Skipper Swede himself. However, since Skipper Swede is like any other sailor and therefore monumentally full of himself and has much more exceptional stories than you or anyone else, a few short accounts follows of Skipper Swede's encounters throughout the years with other wankers of vessels.

Skipper Horror story No1:

I once stood in a very tiny marina, watching a horrible event taking place. My crew and I had already parked up our vessel, and there was only one spot left on the small dock. That is, there was space for a regular size sailboat. Definitely not enough room for the gigantic motor cruiser that came steaming into the harbour.

Without further ado, he dropped anchor and begun to reverse into the slot, while the horrified owners of the two sailboats shouted for king and country that his boat was too big and would not fit. Completely ignoring social manners and all sense of spatial logic, he proceeded to back right in between the sailboats, effectively pushing them out of his way and popping a small chandlery's worth of fenders in the process, stretching stern lines to the point of breaking, and creating a very unsettling grinding noise throughout the whole procedure.

It was a remarkable display of stupidity, all while the skipper of the motorboat shouted back at the shocked sailors that "I'm parking there!", "That's my space" and "I do what I want, because I am the Skipper!"

Yes you are, you wanker.

Skipper Horror story No2:

Now, a lot of yachting people who are involved exclusively in sailboats will automatically object to the previous story and argue that this can be expected from people running motor vessels. If you, dear reader, know little about the yachting scene, it is well worth knowing that there is a silent war between people on sailboats and people on motorboats on a level of similar magnitude to a Middle Eastern conflict.

Sailors think that motorboats are big, noisy and smelly, and that they have no business being on the water. Motor-yachties think that sailboats are slow, in the way, unimportant and that their occupants are a bunch of bohemian organic-eating flower-children who should go back to the 70's. And these two different groups will normally greet each other with a four letter word beginning with 'C' and ending in 'unt'.

However, both groups can be equally bad and actually share more than they think, simply because both groups have vessels operated by skippers. 'Nuff said.

So a story very similar as the one above, happened just a few months later. I was again in a reasonably small marina with only one quayside and there were just two or three spaces left. A gigantic 60 foot catamaran comes screaming into the basin, quickly turns around and starts to reverse into an empty spot. The catamaran is clearly too wide, but this doesn't concern the skipper of the vessel as he slams even more power on the engines and squeezes his way into the slot. The fenders of the neighbouring boats are jumping all over the place, stanchions are bent and one boat is so crunched that the anchor slips and the vessel gets bulldozed right into the concrete quay. The entire transom cracked open, water started pouring into the boat and there was general havoc going on, all while the skipper of the catamaran yelled to everyone that they should move out of his way, that this is his marina and he comes here every week, and that he will call the coastguard and have everyone else pay him a fine.

That guy must indeed have had a really tiny penis.

Skipper Horror story No3:

That sailors are full of themselves is an already established fact, and that the pipe dream of having unparalleled competence is a direct and proportional effect of it. Therefore it can be particularly difficult to offer constructive feedback, suggestions or even a helping hand, as the skipper will by default not need anyone's assistance, recommendations or assessment. This can provoke any person to the point where foam starts building up at the corners of one's mouth, and to the point where the support you intended to offer will be demonstratively absent.

The best example of this is when a boat comes in for berthing and you are ready to help out with the docking procedure. Full of service-mindedness, you shout out the remaining distance to the dock as the boat approaches, getting in position to catch the lines, and then you make the fatal mistake of suggesting "A bit more to your left!"

The instant reply in 99% of the cases is a furious roar of: "Don't tell me how to park my boat!"

Righty-O.

Skipper Horror story No4:

Any flotilla skipper recognises the immense pressure being put on you during the few hours in the afternoon when the herd of cows are coming home. It is a daunting experience to fit more than ten boats in a marina that houses about fifteen, and which already has a few parked up since yesterday. You fidget around on the dock, praying that the sails on the horizon belongs to your crowd and that you will be able to park every single one of them. Then you do another count of boats heading towards the harbour, realise that there are more boats out there than what belongs to you, and you start calling up yours on the VHF to make them hurry up. At the end of it, you've managed to get everyone in safely, and you smirk mischievously as other vessels come in only to turn around and go back out again, as you have secured all the spots with the boats of your flotilla.

That scenario only happens on a good day.

I was once in a very tiny harbour at the hour of madness when everybody's fighting for a parking space. I had, after much stress, managed to get all in, apart from two boats that were apparently enjoying themselves out on the water too much to be bothered to come in and park up. There were only a few spots left, and I was slightly concerned that I wouldn't be able to give them any room if they didn't hurry up. Then an enormous 65-footer screamed in from nowhere and began its parking procedure.

Not wanting to come across as an arsehole, despite my own pressing situation, I decided to give the skipper a hand. It was tight and difficult in the basin, and besides I might just be able to sublimely direct him to the place I wanted him at, instead of him taking the more favourable spots.
"Hello sir, can I help you with your lines?" Big friendly smile on my face. No reply.
"Excuse me sir. Hello? Captain?" He finally turned around and glared at me as if I was Bin Laden standing on the dock.
"Hi there," I continued, "Can I help you with your lines? Are you parking here, or here?" I made a suggestive notion to the spot that suited me better. At that moment he dropped his anchor.

Now, it's worth noting that when you berth stern-to, the appropriate place to make your anchor dig in, is perfectly perpendicular to the dock. Not only is it better in terms of the different forces acting on the boat, it is also more appropriate if you get a wind shift during the night. And if everyone follows this common practise, there will be, quite logically, no crossed anchors in the morning. The dickhead dropped his anchor about five boats to the side, successfully crossing over the anchor chains of the neighbours.

"I'm parking there!" he barked angrily and pierced me with his pig-eyed stare.

"Alright sir," I said, still trying to sound helpful. "I was just wondering, since you dropped your anchor all the way over there."

"What?" he growled, "Are you a *commercial* skipper?" he inquired with the same ferocity. I had at that point had quite enough of this gentleman and replied.

"Matter of fact, I am. Just trying to give a helping hand here." He paused for a moment at my reply, and then came back at me with even more bloodthirstiness.

"Yeah, so am I," he paused for a moment. "So stop your yapping!"

I only wish that instead of walking away, I would have caught his lines only to immediately drop them in the water with an innocent "Ooops, my bad" whilst watching it getting sucked in around the propeller.

Skipper Horror story No5:

During my very early days working in this industry, I had the pleasure of working with a very nice old skipper. He had retired from his normal, land-based profession and had decided to finally pursue his dream of working with boats every day. He had therefore landed the job as a skipper for a charter company cruising around the wonderful Whitsunday islands in Australia, which he thought was a quite a clever way to spend his retirement. I could not agree more.

This gentleman had apparently enjoyed sailing for many years, as he looked like the exact definition of a salty sea-dog. His skin was thicker than the leather of the boots one goes hiking in, and so heavily charcoaled by the sun that he could have been a walking billboard for skin-cancer information. He was more wrinkled than a Chinese Shar-Pei and had a wonderfully inappropriate sense of clothing as he only wore a pair of old and ill-fitting speedos that used to be blue.

The look on the guest's faces when they arrived was priceless.

However, what was even more priceless was his initial welcome-briefing. Due to some legislation in Australia at the time, it was apparently against the law for women to sunbathe topless. But not on his boat it wasn't. That would be against the service to the customers who had paid a lot of money to come out on a holiday and experience some well-deserved freedom and sunshine. So as a treat to the guests, the rule was abolished on his boat and all women were welcome to "hang their tits out", as he so elegantly put it. As long as they didn't tell, he wouldn't either, and they were welcome to show, if not the Full Monty, then at least the big bouncy bits of it. It would be a shame for them to be in such a marvellous paradise-esque place and not get some sunshine on the Norks, Gazongas or Bazookas. But please, dear guests, be aware of the aggressive sunshine here and be sure that you apply plenty of sunscreen lotion, preferably the oily version. It is much more effective.

I swear that this rant of his took up most of the welcome-briefing and that the guest were too shocked to find the ability to oppose this wrinkly and scrawny rotisserie-man sporting his horrible speedos, who managed against all sense of logic to keep a straight face during the whole speech.

Skipper Horror story No6:

One of my first encounters with truly horrible skippers was also when I worked for the previously mentioned charter company. This sad excuse for a human being had taken it upon himself to train the newcomers, particularly the hosts and hostesses, and he did so in such a macabre way that even Hitler would have been impressed. One of his proudest moments, he loudly bragged, was when he managed to make a new, cute, 19-year old hostess with little life- or work experience, cry her eyes out on the first day, have her painfully endure the rest of the mentally castrating trip, and urgently leave the company when they made it back after the 3 days on the charter.

Nice chap.

Working as a host and deckhand for this company, I also had to put up with his Nazi attitude, and I have to admit that it almost broke me. So it was with great joy I received the news that he had been fired, after a serious complaint from the guests. Apparently, it wasn't enough to be a Goering towards his own crew, but he had to have a serious go at the guests as well. After a stream of rude remarks on the first day, and after flipping out over the music the guests wanted to listen to on the second day, they had asked him after lunch if they could make a cup of tea. The reply was along the lines of "No you fucking well can't! Tea is served a 3 PM precisely. You will drink when I tell you to, you will eat when I tell you to and you will swim when I tell you to. So you can shut the fuck up and go sit in the sun or something. I'm busy sailing my boat!"

I think he got away easy by only getting the boot. Getting anally probed by Poseidon's Fork would have been much more appropriate.

Skipper Horror story No7:

Sometimes it is just so outlandish of how unfriendly and unhelpful people can be. One of the many situations when I have experienced this was when I was working as a flotilla skipper a few years ago and had just arrived to the harbour for the day. The tiny harbour was totally empty, save for one small sailboat with a bunch of happy chaps on it, drinking, joking and laughing the afternoon away, and a big catamaran that seemed to be part of a funeral procession. The catamaran had obnoxiously parked himself side-to and right in the bloody middle of the single quay. Not that it mattered at the time, but obviously he had no consideration for boats who might come in a bit later in the afternoon. There was also an underwater ledge on one side of the catamaran, and since he had parked so awkwardly it meant that he had blocked off 5 good spaces in the only area where keelboats could park. Oh well, let's go talk to him. He might be nice.

So we dropped anchor and crept up behind him, on the deep side of the quay. The grey, middle age, on the brink of obese men were all sitting around the cockpit table, staring into their respective drinks, not uttering a word.
"Excuse me? Hi there! How are you gentlemen?" I chirped like an Australian door-to-door salesman. No reply.
"I'm really sorry to bother you gents in your afternoon drink, but may I speak to your skipper?" They uttered a few words in their own language and a short moment later, another man with one foot in the coffin appeared.
"Hello sir, I'm very sorry to disturb you," I said with a smile that could successfully advertise cowshit for toothpaste, "I have a small problem that I was wondering if you could help me with. See, I have a flotilla of 7 more boats coming in and it will be very difficult to fit them all on this side of the quay." He looked totally indifferent as I proceeded, "There is a ledge just on the other side, and the rudders on my boats will get damaged if they park there. So I was hoping that you could possibly move a bit over towards that side of the quay, since you have a catamaran and have a much shallower draught. Your boat will be perfectly safe and you will have plenty of water under your keel and rudder." Still no reaction from the man with a stone face. "Would that be a possibility? You'd still be side-to, and naturally we will assist you to move. It would mean a tremendous amount to me personally if you could help me out here."

"I don't think so," came the answer.

What the bloody hell? I thought to myself and began to explain the whole situation again. His answer was the same, possibly just with a bit more irreverence:

"Not my problem," he said, turned on his heel and walked into the saloon of the catamaran.

I looked at my host who could clearly see that my temper was at its boiling point. Since he spoke the same language as the people on the catamaran, he promptly went over to have a friendly word with them but that didn't help either. We then headed over to the happy boat to let them know that it was going to be packed in the marina, but they were totally fine with it because "The more, the merrier" and yes, upon their arrival they experienced a similarly rude and unmannerly attitude from those arses on the catamaran. "Why do you think we are loudly having such a good time here!?"

After a lot of tweaking, we managed to park up all the boats on the flotilla safely and have a good night's sleep. And as they say; Karma is a bitch:

The following morning, the catamaran departed. Not having particularly good boat handling skills, the permanently irate skipper decided that it was a good idea to get off the dock by putting one engine in forward and the other in reverse. The effect of this is naturally that the boat rotates around the 'Pivot point', which is somewhere in the middle when you look at the boat from above. So if the whole boat is rotating around this point, then the front is inevitably going to the left and the back is going to the right. Right into the dock.

The guys from the happy boat were all standing on the dock, watching the spectacle and loudly cheering and applauding as the catamaran grinded itself off the quay, pulverising the gel-coat on the starboard hull in the process. The host and I were also observing, and although not applauding, we certainly enjoyed the show. When the catamaran was finally clear of the dock, my host turned around to me and said, "Look Swede, I know that we say that all skippers are wankers. But this guy was the wanker of all wankers and there should be a place in hell reserved for people like this. There should be a different nickname or label for that kind of skipper, don't you think?"
I thought for a moment and replied, "Sure, I totally agree. But it will

have to be more prominent than skipper. A more honorary title, like admiral, or commodore or something."

He looked at me with a devilish smile on his face and something wicked burning in his eyes. "I know what we can call them. All the arseholes like this guy."

"Alright, what is it?"

"Captain Cunt!"

Oh, dear.

Accurate description of a skipper

Nautical terms, lesson 4

Spinnaker

An enormous water collecting device that is impossible to retrieve without pre-booking a meeting at the local sail loft. Can be stored everywhere in the boat, all at the same time.

Chart

A navigational aid providing a visual representation of the geography of dry land and topography of the seabed. The only ones ever available, are the ones surrounding the area you are currently sailing.

A list of things to wish

upon a yachting person, who is an idiot.

So with all of the previous said, the proper attitude a sailor should always aspire to employ, is that of being helpful, friendly and supportive. We should all try to assist each other in this industry, because you never know when you might end up in a really crappy situation and be in need of a helping hand yourself. When people arrive to port, you greet them with politeness and a smile as you take their lines, because you know how important that would be when you've been out on the water and arrive to a foreign marina. When someone has a problem, even if it's something as mundane as a piece of cutlery accidentally dropped over the side, you offer your own fork because you know very well how annoying it is to eat your evening dinner of spaghetti with only a spoon. And even when someone is giving you lip, you often take a step back and realise that it might be that the person is stressed out and just needs the troublesome situation resolved. So you swallow it and offer your assistance anyway. Most often they will apologise afterwards and be terribly grateful for your help, when the situation has calmed down.

But there are some people out there on the water who just don't seem to grasp the feeling of community, the brother- and sisterhood of yachting people, or simply how to have a normal and appropriate set of social skills. These are the people who have an attitude of superiority, who look down on others around them and who are complete and utter donkey-bottoms. These people have their heads stuck so far up their own rear that they would need a small tugboat to see daylight again. And naturally it becomes difficult to feel sympathy or wish them well in any situation.

Of course, it's never a good thing to wish misfortune on someone, but when you've had to endure the arrogance, abuse and attitude of some sailors, particularly skippers, it's nice to let off some steam by making a silent and harmless little wish upon them. Normally, these wishes are so gravely horrible and morbid that they provoke uncontrollable laughter, therefore being more therapeutic to your recent nasty experience rather than some kind of magic voodoo towards the people who don't abide by the moral and social codes of sailing.

So as you view through these following little invocations, my dear reader, I urge you to unravel each one at a time and genuinely visualise the situation they describe, and particularly the outcome that will follow with the same inevitability as a rumbly tummy after a big Indian curry night.

- May you not find a berthing space in your next harbour. Ever.
- May your batteries stay flat forever.
- May the bed-bugs from a thousand skanky charter mattresses infest your genitalia.
- May half of your charter guests be permanently sea-sick. Down below.
- May the other half be permanently sea-sick. On you.
- May your stern lines always get caught in your propellers.
- May your tidal calculations be excessively cumbersome, and the result always slightly off. On the minus-side.
- May your halyards snap inside of the mast.
- May your anchors always locate and get permanently entangled in that pile of rubble, old wreck or particularly difficult rock on the bottom, 20 meters down.
- May your cabin hatches be inadvertently left ever so slightly open while you are underway.
- May your fuel tank and freshwater tank get mixed up during filling up.
- May your boat papers always be out of date.

And finally my utmost favourite...

- May your waste tanks explode!

Nautical terms, lesson 5

Duck:

1.   A semi-aquatic bird that usually hangs around in marinas and which produces an impressive amount of excrement on jetties, quays, and on the outside seating of the local yacht club.

2.   A key ingredient of a traditional Chinese dish. Most likely invented by a marina-based restaurant owner.

3.   A word preceding the halfway motion of horizontal part of rigging traversing the centreline of the boat. Usually exclaimed too late.

On charter guests

So even though Skipper Swede has been ferociously insulting and obnoxiously mocking sailors and skippers alike, and doing so with remarkable excitement, it is worth remembering that he might just be equally passionate in taking the piss. Not all sailors are full of themselves, by far, and not all skippers are wankers, by a mile. Most of us involved in the boating scene are actually quite nice, pleasant, humble and cool people. Naturally, this translates just the same to all the folks that we get to meet while being involved in this profession. Charter guests are in general a very wonderful bunch, happy and high-spirited as they are on an adventurous holiday, and it's easy to socialise and befriend new individuals. But then you also have the minority; all the awful people we have the misery to deal with during any random working hours.

Nowadays the charter guests are just as diverse as the crowd on an audition for MasterChef, with background and experience to match. Gone are the days when sailors and sailors alone came out for a sailing vacation. This is in many ways fantastic, as countless of delightful people get to experience the wonderful time of a holiday on the water, something that was very difficult to do back in the days. Reasonably inexperienced sailors can now bring their families and friends on an exciting and relaxing trip, and thanks to both RYA and the design development of yachts, they can make it work without too much hassle and be safe in quite punishing conditions. That is some fabulous development, as many more have been invited to enjoy the enchantment of sailing, and as it has been demystified to be neither exclusively for the rich nor the circumnavigators.

But this development has also brought the odd rotten egg into the Easter-basket of treats, and Skipper Swede could not write a book like this without including the priceless stories about some of the shockingly daft charter guests he has met whilst slaving away in this industry. Read and weep.

Boot out of hell

So there I was, going out for a week as the charter skipper for a family of mum, dad and three kids. Three boys. Three very unruly boys.

"My, oh my," I thought to myself when I read through the manifest describing the upcoming week at work. It was not going to be easy. And frankly, these kids deserve a chapter, if not a whole book, to themselves. But so does the dad, whose remarkably modest intelligence and social manners seemed to have been divided between his horrendous offspring. Without mincing my words here, he was certainly walking the parade, but on a different street. And his kids were doing the same, in another town.

However, being a clever boy and responsible skipper, I was determined to give them a great time and show them a fantastic sailing vacation. I should have earned a medal for my professionalism, as the week probably turned out to be the absolutely worst charter week of my life, facing me with existential questions ranging from the art of parenting to the destiny of the human race. But again, that can indeed be retold in another book. Or much better; not at all, as my subconscious has done a fantastic job in repressing the entire memory, save the following extraction:

On the day before last, I decided that I'd had enough of their company and literally sprinted off the dock as soon as we had arrived and found, with remarkable speed, an obscure bar to take refuge in for the evening. Around nine at night I made it back to the boat; it was entirely abandoned, filled with silence and radiating harmony from the lack of its horrible inhabitants of the week. I promptly went in to my cabin and shut the door, figuring that at least I would be able to relax for a few hours before the guests made it back from dinner.

At nine-fifteen, I was disturbed by children's yelling from the quayside. Not the normal kind of yelling as one would imagine, with words that forms some sort of sentence and are in a remote way an attempt of communication. And not the one that children so often use where random words of importance are loudly incorporated with the game they are involved in playing. No, instead I had the privilege to listen to wordless and morbid screams from these joyful rascals, who had also managed to gather the rest of the kids in the marina for a deafening display in auditory suicide.

Should have stayed in the bar then.

At around eleven, after a good two and a half hours of this non-stop screaming insanity, the parents arrived to the quayside, quite on the unsteady side after supper and plenty of after-dinner drinks. Without further ado, the kids of all vessels were immediately and forcefully put to bed and a tiny shimmer of hope flickered momentarily in my ghetto-blasted brain. After all, the parents were quite drunk and they might just call it a night.

Wrong. The better idea was to have a cockpit party. On our boat.

Mind you that on a Jeanneau Sun Odyssey 439, as it is on many other modern boats built for charter, the aft cabins are located immediately underneath the cockpit seats. And my cabin happened to be the aft starboard one. Marvellous.

So the horrendous evening continued on, and quite frankly, the only difference between the behaviour of the parents and the previous parade of adolescent retards on the dock, was that every now and then an understandable word or two snuck in to the attempted and sad excuse for a conversation they were having.

This went on until three in the morning, upon when I decided to get out of my cabin and get some air. Unfortunately, I had not realised that the gene-pool failure of a dad had not gone to bed like the others had, but was still up emptying the last of whatever was left in the sea of bottles in the cockpit. And as one does when one is drunk and has had a pleasant evening, he started chatting with whomever was around which was, quite naturally, only me. He did this for a good hour, using the exact same sentence over and over again, neither producing any alternate ways of convincing me of something I was not even interested in, nor actually getting anywhere in his abominable rant. Just before four in the morning, he finally left me alone, the expected heavy weather blew in, and all skippers including myself were up for the rest of the morning making sure that fenders were protecting and anchors holding in place.

That was not the worst part.

About an hour after they had all staggered back to the boat, and therefore also an hour into the adult's rendering of 'Which imbecile can make the best impersonation of the mating call of an oversexed moose', the dad felt terribly comfortable with both hosting his new-found friends on 'his' yacht, and with his own immensely delightful and witty persona, and decided to make himself even a bit more relaxed and free-spirited. So he leant back in his seat and dramatically kicked off his flip flops. One bounced loudly on the wall somewhere in the cockpit floor, the other shot as a projectile from the hell that was his nasty, sweaty and smelly feet, right through the tiny porthole of the starboard aft cabin and landed with all its repulsive and vomit-inducing odour, gravel and god knows what else, with a dramatic and satisfying smack, right on my face.

If it wasn't for the sheer surprise of this new event, I could at that point have rolled over in bed and started to cry. Instead, I aggressively returned the flip flop the way it came and made good effort to do so with the same speed. A rugby player could not have produced a better throw. I'm reasonably sure that it made it all the way overboard and floated away, as the dad asked around for it the following morning and it was never to be seen again.

The weather that had blown in during the very early morning hours kept on, and the following day offered a good force 6-7 with 8 in the gusts, and I was damned if I would reef the sails.

A melting pot of food culture

Many times have I listened to the happy buzz from guests who are tremendously glad to be on a sailing holiday. They are away in a non-native country, having fantastic adventures foreign to their everyday grind, and essentially experiencing the trip of a lifetime. It feels great to be part of the team that makes someone's hard-earned, well-spent and much-anticipated vacation a success. And not only is it a good sensation when you know that you've done your job well, but an even bigger satisfaction to see the guests feeling ecstatic and overwhelmed by their experience.

In other words; it is great for everyone, including yourself, to make other people happy. If you didn't know, Skipper Swede doubles on odd weekends as a do-gooder philosopher and philanthropist.

However, the gratification one gets from making people happy is sometimes terribly absent, and sometimes entirely unachievable. There are some seriously bitter people in this world whose idea of a good time is in finding the faults and shortcomings of pretty much everything they encounter. And it would be easier to trap a fart in a storm, than to make them appreciate the uniqueness and diversity of the local place. This is not a specific occurrence just in the yachting scene; I've had the misfortune to meet such people everywhere imaginable during my travels and through work. But regardless the circumstance, you always get flabbergasted by their audacity and disrespect for other cultures and countries, and start wondering why some people bother leaving the little shitholes they call home in the first place.

The first time I experienced this was in the wonderful town of Biarritz in southern France in a situation entirely unrelated to sailing. I had met some fellow countrymen, a couple from a Swedish city further up north, and we had decided to hang out for the day. As I was travelling by myself, I thought this was a remarkably good idea. Whilst chilling on the comfortable main beach in town, Grand Plage, I noticed a few odd remarks from both of them which I decided to overlook on the assumption that they were a) joking, b) having a profoundly poor sense of humour, or c) being complete twats. I was unsure of which category they belonged to, so I waited in respect of the newfound potential friendship. I needed not to wait for long, as their rotten announcements became more frequent and showed a formidable impoliteness to the city and country hosting them. There is no need to retell all of their nonsense here; I left their little party when they had successfully gone through the faults of the French history, culture, food, people and politics, and then in lack of anything else to complain about, advanced onto the inane architecture in this supposedly third-world country.

Of all things to whine about, you choose Architecture? Only utterly sad characters would do that. But that was my first time of meeting 'complainers' and certainly not my last, particularly not in the field of yachting, and especially not when it comes to food. Complaining about food is a much more practicable process as most people eat several times a day, and the object of fuss is served on a platter half a meter in front of you. But nonetheless, this kind of wailing classifies as equally mentally retarded as bitching about architecture.

I once sat in a Greek tavern with some of my guests who made a point of continuously complaining about their dining experience in real time. If it wasn't objections about the horrendous food that the proprietor brought out from the kitchen, it would instead be about the said idiot of a proprietor whose idiotic menu didn't offer the special grub suiting their palette. And while they devoured their main course with great appetite, they were simultaneously giving the whole idiotic country of Greece, with its 6000-or-so islands, some stick and croaked about how every single idiotic restaurant had exactly the same menu and how utterly bored they were of Moussaka and Pork-In-The-Bag.

There is a fast-food chain with golden arches in THAT direction that might suit you better, you cretin.

Now, I can appreciate that it gets terribly monotonous having, for example, a Greek salad to every single meal. Especially when you live and work in the country. Even though everything was invented in Greece, or at least so the Greeks would like to believe, creating a Greek salad is neither the culinary equivalent to being a rocket scientist, nor does it qualify as more interesting than studying the mating rituals of freshwater mussels. Think about it (no, not the mussels). Tomatoes, cucumbers, red onion and olives with a fat slab of feta cheese on top, swimming in a generous sea of olive oil? Hardly a culinary treat worth revisiting more than once a year. But is it worth moaning about? Only if you are a real asshole.

I once dined in Greece with a guest who normally lived in Central America. He had ordered a Special Seafood Platter which was quite a unique dish for the area and I had never seen it in any other tavern around. Everything was catch of the day and so fresh that if it was a pork steak it would still be singing Hakuna Matata.

It came out as a gorgeous mountain of treats from Poseidon himself with a variety of clams, mussels, octopus, squid, cuttlefish, shrimps, crabs, lobster meat and different kinds of fish. Needless to say, I was thoroughly impressed and glanced with remorse on my own plate containing a sad brick of chicken in some random lemon sauce with undercooked rice on the side. *What a treat this gentleman was in for*, I thought to myself, *He will be terribly pleased*. But no. After digging through half of his spectacular platter of Fruits de la Mer, a symphony of nit-picking emerged from him. But not a normal symphony orchestrated by a mixture of instruments, but rather one single monotonous tone like the one you hear when someone hangs up the phone on you. This tone consisted of him repeating himself in the exact same way about the very insult put onto him, of the restaurant cutting up the various seafood in sizable chunks. Where he now lived, somewhere in Central America, the local chefs would chop it up in thinner slices. Apparently, he was too blockheaded to use his own knife and fork to achieve the same result. As his rant went on for the better part of the evening, he successfully managed to declare his horrible dining experience personally to every single one of the 35 individuals at the table. In each incarnation of his harangue he would, at least three times, make sure that the receiver properly understood that chefs in Central America would 'Chop it up'. He also followed up this claim each time by making a mysterious gesture that would either signify a person energetically sandpapering the palm of his hand, or possibly a very powerful combat technique performed by a Ninja.

After significantly less than 35 times, I swore that I'd chop him up if I heard it one more time.

Now, we have all been served a poor meal, been to low-quality restaurants and experienced worse service than you would expect from Fawlty Towers. And it is in everyone's rights to have negative opinions, as one should definitely be able to expect a certain level of quality in a restaurant. After all, you are paying for a service and the very core idea of any restaurant is to be specialised in that service in contrast to, say, a prison camp. But with that said, there is a grand difference between passing judgement on what actually matters, i.e. the food and service provided, and to piss and moan for the sake of pissing and moaning. The latter is just a stubborn unwillingness to embrace other cultures and a refusal of accepting that things are different outside of your tiny bubble. Because at the end of the day, why would a foreign place offer something that is native to your origin?

So a little piece of advice: If you are going to complain about other's shit when you are abroad, stay at home!

The important bits on a boat

Most charter companies have something called a 'Hand over', 'Boat briefing' or similar. This is in essence a rundown of everything on the boat so that the charter guest will know the workings of the specific vessel, and it also works as a bit of a barometer for the capabilities of the guest in question. One can normally get a psychic premonition of a guest's upcoming trip across the nearest reef when conversing with them during the briefing.

Skipper Swede does pride himself with an extensively thorough boat briefing and think that it's only fair that a guest that has paid so much money for the vessel, who faces the changeable elements and weather, who might not have the knowledge of someone who does it for a profession, and who might not have been out on a boat for a whole year, should only be given as much support as possible. The boat is gone over properly, and so is the navigation and destinations for their trip. Normally this proceeds very effortlessly and the guests are as a rule quite grateful for the information they receive. However, every now and then, a wanker comes along and ruins what was up until then a great day at work.

One of the most arrogant ones I came across was a woman who demonstratively did not pay attention to my briefing. The only few times she did show some interest, was to argue against my explanations and to point out that she had superior knowledge and experience of pretty much everything that had to do with sailing. She then proceeded to successfully sail the boat aground on the first day, hitting the only navigational hazard in a 15 nautical mile radius, enroute to the first destination. Luckily, that set the tone for the rest of the week as humility sprung up as quickly as a venereal disease in a brothel, and she remained pleasantly soft-spoken for the rest of the trip. However, on the last day, all the boats had made it in to the dock at five in the afternoon, our deadline for arrival. Except for this one. Not that we were too surprised, and we joked amongst ourselves that perhaps they had run aground again. At six we started to get a bit confused and began asking around the other boats, especially the ones that came in last, but no one had seen them. We tried the VHF and the phone, but to no avail. Finally, at around eight, we managed to hunt them down, and it turned out that her navigational skills had been so exceptionally inaccurate, that not only had they missed the harbour, but the whole bloody island as well and continued a good 20 NM north.

So the outcome of the navigation briefing can become quite absurd, and likewise it can be immensely infuriating when one explains the various features on the boat and the guests still cock it up. Mind you, these are guests who are supposed to have procured one of the many certifications available. The whole point of these certifications is that they actually guarantee the holder is a skilful yachts-person who should be able to navigate, understand the rules of the road and have a reasonable knowledge of the parts of a sailing vessel, amongst other things. However, more than once I've found that these certified sailors probably got the ticket out of a cereal box.

One example of this was when I made a briefing on a 43-footer with in-mast furling. Now, I'm not a big fan of this system for starters as it normally gives a horrendous sail shape and can create more problems than it solves. But it was on the boat whether I liked it or not, and it had to be demonstrated and explained. So during the briefing, the following dialogue took place:

"So when you furl the mainsail out, you open both jammers and pull on the rope this way," I said. The sail came out by a meter and a half. "I see," the guest said.
"Good, and to furl it in, simply pull the other rope while keeping a bit of tension on this one. That makes a nice and tight furl, and prevents it from jamming in the slit on the mast." I showed again and the sail rolled in.
"Right, got it. Can I try?" He positioned himself at the rope and folded down both jammers and started pulling for king and country.
"Now, why do you think this doesn't work?" I asked calmly. "It's because the jammer is down. As I mentioned, it needs to be in the up position. Up means open. You can only pull when it's open." I opened it up and the sail came out by a good two meters. "Right, shall we pull it back in?"
"Ok," he said chirpily and folded both jammers down and started pulling like a maniac. Naturally nothing happened.
"As I said, you need to have the jammers open," I said and did my best to sound helpful and supportive.
"So both jammers needs to be closed when you pull it out?"
"No, they need to be open."

"Ok… And when you pull it in, they should be closed?"

"No, they need to be open then as well."

"I see. So when you pull it out, one is closed and the other open?"

"No, just… just open both. Regardless of what you are doing, open both jammers."

"So… I don't get it. When I pull in, I have the right jammer down, yes?"

"No, look, have both jammers open when you roll the sail out, and when you roll it in." I demonstrated again. "And just control the furling with tension on the two ropes." He looked perplexed.

"So let's say I want to go on a starboard tack. Then I should have the port one open?"

"No, of course not. If you are sailing, the jammers are closed," I said while my brain felt as if it was turning to slush and dripping out my ears.

"But when I'm tacking, I want to pull the sail to the other side, so then they should be open."

"Ehm…what? The furling lines has nothing to do with the sheet lines. That's two separate operations. When you furl or roll the sail, keep both open. When you are done rolling in or out, close them down."

"Ok, got it!" he said and slammed down both jammers and started to pull.

"No, no… hang on… look," I said and started over again.

This went on for a good 20 minutes, and in the end it seemed that the guest understood the mechanics of it. But apparently they had some problems getting the sail back in on the first day already. So instead of figuring out what caused the problem, i.e. a closed jammer, they decided to put the furling rope on a winch and grind the sucker back in, resulting in the whole rope snapping like a shoelace on a pair of ancient deck shoes drenched in saltwater. That line should hold for many, many tonnes, so it's a godsend that they didn't winch the whole mast off the boat in the process.

So one can well see that these situations are deeply infuriating and that anyone who is subjected to these circumstances will go bald or grey-haired with remarkable swiftness. After all, one is there to do a job, a job one takes a striking amount of pride in. One would enjoy a tiny amount of respect for the craft, and therefore one naturally has some expectations of the guests. Not a lot of expectations, but just simple and basic ones that don't make you scream friendly things like *'Oy! Pay Attention To This!'*, *'You Can Bloody Well Listen When*

I'm Talking!', and *'How Come You Don't Know The Flippin' Basics Of Sailing?'* But then again, I have come to the point where I have almost given up on my expectations.

I was once interrupted during a critical part of a briefing, while covering the various personal safety features on the boat. The skipper had wandered off to the forward cabin and come back to the briefing, holding up a piece of cloth.

"…in case of great emergency. This button sends out a digital signal which is then picked up by…"

"What is this?" she interrupted.

"Uhm, what?" I responded and homed in on the new item of interest.

"Oh, nothing, I'm just wondering what this is," she said casually.

What the fuck? I thought to myself and quickly regained my composure: "That, is a wind scoop." I could have sworn that my left eyebrow lifted on its own accord.

"Ah, ok. What does it do?"

Well, it serves no purpose when you are issuing a mayday and are about to die, I thought to myself and responded: "As the name suggests, it scoops down wind. You normally hang it at the front hatch and it cools down the boat at night."

"Oh, what a great thing," she said joyfully. "Can we put it up now?"

No we bloody well can't!

What world? Oh, your world.

One of the lovely guests I once had on flotilla was a self-made entrepreneur and business man. To his defence, he did have a good heart and was not a bad person, he was simply just not living on the same planet as the rest of us. This was one of those characters you meet in life and instantly realise that he is operating on his own internal agenda. A prime example of a person who not only has formed a retort before you even open your mouth, but who finds it more important to respond to his own enquiry than waiting for someone else to have a go. Someone who effectively is arguing with himself and always wins the debate, and who must have a mechanical failure with the workings of the ear as his own voice is the only thing he hears.

He was, in spite of this weird trait, quite a sociable person, in his own awkward way. "Why is that," one might wonder, and the reason was simply the topics of monologue that came up as soon as he initiated his rhapsody in retard. To have to listen to the story behind why the gentleman could not make his wife pregnant is not one of the first things that spring to mind for a gregarious blubber.

To say that he was socially ungraceful would be a tremendous understatement, and one of the best episodes happened when he wandered into a café where all the charter staff hung out. After absentmindedly saying hi to us, he walked up to my friend who worked there. Without any pleasantries, he asked her for a scouring pad, as the kettle on his boat was dirty. Perplexed, she replied that he could get one from the charter company itself, or why not in the supermarket next door, but why on earth would he ask in a café? The answer was simply that he knew that she would be there and, well, since she was a woman, she must therefore have scouring pads. He was happy to clean the kettle himself though.

He left with astonishing speed as she furiously chased him out of the café, while her husband, a fellow skipper I was having coffee with, laughed so hard that he could barely breathe.

How to be a moron with all the bells and whistles

I once came in to a marina a bit earlier than usual. I was skippering a boat for two clients, father and son, and they really wanted to experience the town we had arrived in. So as they were off exploring I had nothing to do and decided to help out on the quayside as other boats started to fill up the harbour. The flotilla crew were very appreciative as they had a good dozen boats coming in, apparently with some quite demanding clients.

Been there.

After about three hours of very tricky direction and man-handling of the boats, the whole flotilla was in and clients enjoying themselves with gin & tonics in the cockpits under the pleasant Mediterranean sun. Then the flotilla skipper came up to me.

"Hey Swede, thanks for your help today. Really appreciate it."

"No problems man, glad I could help. You seem to have your hands full this week."

"Tell me about it," he said and paused for a second. "Actually, could I ask for your help in something else as well?"

"Sure, what's up?"

"You will love this," he said and grinned. "Follow me."

We headed down the dock and up to one of the boats in the flotilla. The customer stood awkwardly on the cockpit roof with a boathook. I glanced to the flotilla skipper.

"I'll let you handle this one," he said. "I can't talk to this jerk anymore today."

So I put on my best customer-care face and approached the guy on the boat. "Hi there, what seems to be the problem?" I asked with the chirpiness of a hamster on crack.

"Oh, hi yourself," the client said absent-mindedly. "Well, I have a problem with the main halyard."

"Alright, nothing we cannot fix," I replied and located the halyard. It was swinging about, three quarters up the mast. "How did you manage to get it all the way up there?" I said slightly confused.

"Well, I forgot to attach it to the sail. Then I pulled," he said.

"Yeah, but it's a long way up. Surely you must have realised that it wasn't attached to the sail as soon as you started pulling?"

"Yes I did"

"So how did it end up all the way there?"
"Well, I couldn't reach it with the boathook, so I figured that if I pulled a bit more, it might loosen up and come down by itself."

As Einstein so eloquently put it: "Two things are infinite. The Universe and Human Stupidity. And I'm not too sure about the Universe".

What goes on in the mind of a skipper
when dealing with charter guests, who are idiots

Charter guest:
"What happens to the island during a hurricane? Does it float away?"
Skipper:
"You are an idiot."

Charter guest:
"How many islands are there in Greece?"
Skipper:
"Do I look like a flipping encyclopaedia, you idiot?"

Charter guest:
"Can you swim underneath the island?"
Skipper:
"You are an idiot."

Charter guest:
"I want to sail to Athens, Mykonos, Skiathos, Santorini, Crete and Rhodes this week!"
Skipper:
"You are an idiot."

Charter guest:
"Why do black people in the Caribbean speak French?"
Skipper:
"Seriously?? You are an idiot."

Charter guest:
"Should I go to the bathroom now or later?
Skipper:
"Is it urgent? Is it number one or number two? Either way, I'm not your da-da, and you are an idiot."

Charter guest:
"Which star is that?"
Skipper:
"That's the masthead anchor light, you idiot."

Charter guest:
"I didn't know there were fish in the water here."
Skipper:
"Actually, we put them there to entertain the kids. You idiot."

Charter guest:
"What can I eat while I'm on the boat?"
Skipper:
"Only apples. Idiot."

Charter guest:
"Are there pirates around here?"
Skipper:
"You are looking at one, you idiot."

Charter guest:
"So Swede, where are you from again? Denmark? Finland? All those countries are the same anyway."
Skipper Swede:
"No, I'm actually from Djibouti. What do you think, you idiot?"

Charter guest:
"Blablabla, blabla, blablablabla, bla bla bla, blabla blabla blabla, blablablabla"
Skipper:
"You still don't get it, do you?"

Dear reader, say what you want about this little section in the book. However, I urge you to read it again, and this time keep in mind that Skipper Swede and his compadres have actually had each and every question or statement posed onto them in the past. Literally and without editing for dramatic effect. There is, in other words, little or no hope for humanity.

So a pirate walks into a bar. The scruffy ol' seadog limps in on his wooden peg-leg to an empty bar stool, peers with his only good eye on the barman and orders a large scotch. The barman puts the drink down on the bar and the old man grabs the glass with his left hand and puts his right, hooked hand, on the counter. The barman, intrigued, starts a conversation.

"So, I've bet you've been through a lot out there, old man," the barman says.

"Aye. Been out through the most," the gruffy old man replies.

"Been through a few battles?"

"Aye. Lost me leg in the fierce battle outside Grenada," said the salty old guy. "The powder magazine exploded and ripped it right off!"

"Seen a few sea creatures as well, I suppose?"

"Aye. Lost me right hand to the Kraken itself," the old shellback mused. "Bit it right off as I struggled with his blasted tentacles!"

"Crikey!" the barman exclaimed with impression, "and what happened with your eye?"

"Aye"

"Yes, what happened to your eye?"

"Oh, me eye? Got drenched by a rogue wave during a hurricane."

"What? You lost your eye by getting some seawater in it?"

"Aye, bit unlucky on the first day with me hook".

- Courtesy of some random website with quite shitty sailing jokes.

"There's nothing... absolutely nothing... half so much worth doing as messing about in boats."

- *Kenneth Grahame, The Wind In The Willows*

Nautical terms, lesson 6

Pilotage
The skill of locating and making physical contact with every sandbar, reef, buoy, marker, pontoon or concrete pier in the comfortable visual proximity of the Yacht Club on a busy day.

Life Jacket
A buoyancy aid designed as fashion statement, effectively making you look like the happy Orange Michelin Man.

On Terminology

Have you ever thought about the different words and phrases that one may come across in the marine language? There is a very distinct terminology to describe various facets of the yachting life, and if it wasn't for the fact that the foundation of this jargon is so remarkably similar to English, it could almost be a language on its own.

Sailors are very proud of the marine terminology. It makes them stand out from the rest of the low-life landlubbers. They can communicate with each other in a way that sounds like gibberish for the uninitiated, and therefore keep everyone in the dark concerning their intentions. And since people who do not speak this secret language always have to ask the meaning of different words, sailors automatically have the upper hand in any conversation and manages to achieve authority on their proficiency of the terminology alone.

As mentioned before, sailors are quite full of themselves.

However, it can be very interesting to study where all the various words come from. Take the most basic example of Port and Starboard. Legend has it that on the ancient ships, particularly the Viking ships (which pleases Skipper Swede since Skipper Swede is, well, a Swede), the rudder was located on the right side of the boat. Therefore that side, or board, would be where one would steer from. Hence "Styr-Bord" in Swedish, translated to "Steer-Board" in English, which developed in to "Starboard", possibly influenced by Dutch. Port on the other hand, most likely came from the fact that boats with the rudder on the right side always had to berth the quayside with their left-side to. The left side was then, quite logically, where one would disembark and offload cargo, and the cargo would go straight into the massive doors of the warehouse, which are also knows as ports (also avec dans la Francais incroyable et merveilleuse, la Port).

So after this little lovely piece of linguistic history lesson, one can very well find that the terminology of the marine industry can be quite entertaining and interesting. However, as mentioned earlier, the industry with its sailors can be quite retarded in the use of the marine terminology.

For starters, have you any idea how hard it is to learn all the words of sailing, not just in your own language, but in a new one as well? When Skipper Swede took his qualifications (RYA courses are naturally held in English), he thought that terminology would be the least of his worries. But alas, how wrong he was! All the sailing terms from the Swedish language had to be re-learnt in English. And do you think the words were the same? Of bloody course not! Let's again make a simple example and re-use the term 'Port'. In Swedish, the word describing left on a boat is 'Babord'. Somehow I fail to see how these two words describing the same thing can come from the same linguistic origin. So not only is sailing terminology a secret language in your own tongue, but secret to any other nation's yachting community as well. Sometimes I wonder if people just make shit up as they go along.

And then we have these self-absorbed sailing-folks. I was a long time ago lectured by a lovely skipper who found it terribly enjoyable to point out that I didn't know anything about sailing. We were at a party and he made a big show of letting everyone know that I didn't understand any of the terms he challenged me with. "Do you know what a 'luff' is? Or a 'leech'?" he asked. "Of course not, because you don't know anything about boats!"

Ehm. Right.

At the point when I thought that Mr Arrogant Bastard should be quiet and return to the little cave he crawled out from, I happily encouraged him to continue the derogatory lecture when he had learned to speak Swedish. Particularly, when he had learned the Swedish marine terminology. To my great enjoyment, that statement created a thunderous laughter from the others at the party. The crowd went wild, as it were. And so did Skipper Swedes' ego.

There was another situation where a very good friend of mine thought it terribly funny that I didn't use the proper terminology. For example, I would say 'Park a boat' instead of 'Berthing' or 'Docking'. And I would refer to a Mooring buoy as a ball. My friend simply could not believe that a certified commercial skipper and instructor alike, would use such incorrect marine terminology when he himself, not having any qualifications except from some brief service in the Navy, would use all the proper words.

I kindly asked him if a mooring ball wasn't in fact still a ball, regardless of how he liked to call it. Granted, sometimes it has the shape of a cone, octahedron or bi-cone, but you have to admit that it sounds slightly convoluted to tell your crew to pick up the mooring-octahedron. And furthermore, regardless if you are on the water, in the air or on land, you still park your vessel. No need to get fancy-schmancy on me.

By the way, when it comes to the English use of the word 'Buoy', you might want to tread carefully in your pronunciation. You have the option of either pronouncing it as 'Boy' or as 'Bu-ee'. Personally, I prefer the latter as "Let's go over there and pick up that boy" doesn't sound particularly professional, unless you have the hots for Roger The Cabin Boy.

Naturally, my friend did not agree with neither 'Parking' or 'Ball', so I proceeded to tell him the following story that had happened to me during my Yacht Master Power exam.

My examiner was a grumpy old geezer. Apparently, this gentleman was one of the highest ranking examiners in the RYA organisation, and on top of that he also ran his own sailing school and had logged enough miles to get from earth to the nearest galaxy. And as so many examiners, he radiated an air of dislike and disbelief, and the three of us thought from the start that we would all fail within an hour.

Luckily, he turned out to be a very pleasant man, at least after you passed the exam, and he would then tell fascinating stories about his sailing adventures all over the world and share tips and tricks that only a very seasoned mariner would know of. And during most of those stories, he used highly improper terminology. Naturally, we noticed this and glanced sideways to each other in confusion. Did he really say that? An examiner? Was he still testing us?

So at the end of the exam, after we had all passed and the nervousness and tension had subsided, we decided to ask him.
"Sir, excuse me, we all have a question?"
"Sure, go ahead."
"Why do you insist on using... ehm... shall we say 'incorrect' terminology?"
"Ah, you mean why I say 'Map' instead of 'Chart'?"
"Yes, for example. We were a bit confused about that."

"There is a simple reason to it," he said with an air of superiority. "I have a lifelong experience on the water. I am an instructor and an examiner. I run my own sailing school." He paused for a moment and fixed us all with his scrutinizing stare. "And there are two reasons: For starters, it means the same bloody thing. And second, I will say 'Map' just because I can!"

That man deserves a medal!

On tidal calculations

"I sat down on the uncomfortable and uninviting steel chair in the badly fluorescent lit place. The air in the bunker-like room was saturated with the repulsive stench of old sweat and sailors salt-infused wet-weather gear, and the room held such a horrendous aroma that my stomach wanted to turn itself inside out. Many mariners had come to this god-awful place in the past, facing the same nightmarish terror that was now spread out in front of me. Icing cold shivers rippled down my spine, as I feverishly grabbed the pen and ruler out of my box of tricks, and with shaking hands and fighting the urge to have today's lunch return the way it came in and spray the nautical charts on the table, I reached for the thick Almanac and flicked up the appropriate page, and began to do the required secondary port tidal calculation."

This lovely little extract describes quite literally what Skipper Swede experienced during various YachtMaster trainings in Falmouth, UK. And it is also what so many other fellow sailors have had to painfully endure during either their courses, their private sailing life, their professional sailing life, or even their life of instructing and training new aspiring sailors.

Secondary port tidal calculations. What a joke.

There are some wonderful activities that you could do instead of tidal calculations. Almost everything you do will be tremendously more worthwhile and more rewarding than wasting several hours calculating secondary ports.

Don't get me wrong, knowing what the tide is supposed to do and when it's doing it is information not to be taken lightly. You might run your vessel aground if you don't take the tides seriously. You might also add several hours to your journey, beating against the tidal stream if you ignore the importance of tides. But that is not the issue here, is it? No, it's the fact that you are manually calculating the tides.

Think about it. As Skipper Swede is writing this chapter, it's already in the beginning of the 21'st century. Who in their right minds would ever attempt to manually calculate tides on a secondary port in this day and age? There are computer programs, software and apps that will do that for you. But some people seem to be under the delusion that there is a romantic notion in doing it manually. Unfortunately for them, that reasoning is just a really sad excuse of trying to convince other sailors that your stone-age methods should still be used, and that you are in fact really proficient at making a fire with a flint instead of using your flame-thrower. There is no romantic notion in calculating tidal variations! None! You want romance? Read a shitty novel. You want romanticism at sea? Visit a brothel when arriving to port. Doing these calculations is simply a waste of time, and you will tend to find that after several hours of straining your brain, you will most often get it wrong anyway. Let me emphasise this: Manual calculation is a joke!

An example of this was when Skipper Swede sailed through the Messina Straight. This particular passage is quite entertaining and provides a reasonable bit of traffic. Therefore it's truly important to get your tidal calculations right, so that you are not making 6 knots against a 5 knot tidal current, at the moment when you try to avoid that big bloody tanker heading your way.

The whole crew, including the skipper, had spent the previous day making calculations backwards and forwards until our brains felt like they had just been through a marathon of 'The Bold and the Beautiful'. The presentation was utterly amusing, as every single one of the individual calculations were at least an hour off to each other, and we had therefore no clue of when our tidal window would happen. The skipper, quite fast on his feet, grabbed a local fisherman that had just arrived and asked him for some insight. The weather-beaten old geezer shrugged his shoulders and told us to go through at mid-day, which no-one had yet suggested. Naturally, he was entirely right. The sad group of well-educated yachtmasters that we were, dressed in fancy foul-weather-gear and carrying expensive yachting kit, standing around looking like a right bunch of twats, had all been wrong. And that despite our many hours of calculations, our eagerness to solve the problem, and most of all, in spite of that we actually found it entertaining to waste all that time and effort in getting some hideously incorrect answers.

So, anyone who finds tidal calculations interesting, exciting or intriguing should get out more. Alternatively, they should attempt to get laid, which is in itself a consequence of getting out more.

Naturally, there is a good point in knowing how to make these calculations and to understand the methods, but as soon as your level of expertise is up to scratch, you should instantly revert to a software. So the tip-of-the-day is that you should learn how it works, and when you are good enough you should use a program, an electronic device, or have a student to do it for you. As a matter of fact, don't use the student, as the student is human and will get it wrong, rendering you and the yacht aground.

Here are a few jolly examples of things to do instead of tidal calculations:

• Read a book
• Write a book
• Listen to music
• Learn to play the violin
• Learn to play the violin on a night watch
• Masturbate (whilst looking into a mirror if you are the skipper)
• Masturbate loudly on a night watch
• Conjure up a new wind-up to annoy your ship mates
• Look at the stars (night) or the horizon (day)
• Masturbate loudly on a day watch
• Have an apple
• Have a Bentos pie, the true meal of a sailor
• Use the heads
• Use the heads while learning to play the violin, on a night watch

Nautical terms, lesson 7

Tide
Astrophysical phenomenon resulting in previously submerged reefs coming awash. Any vessel's grounding can later be calculated with great accuracy.

Current
Flow of a body of water. Designed to always originate from your current destination. Hence the name.

Grounding
The art of unexpectedly performing hull maintenance on your boat.

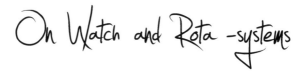

On Watch and Rota -systems

When you are doing a delivery job, or even out cruising with your family, it is quite important to set up a working watch system or a rota that every crew member can follow. The fifth rule in the COLREGS stipulates that *'Every vessel shall at all times maintain a proper look-out by sight and hearing as well as by all available means appropriate in the prevailing circumstances and conditions so as to make a full appraisal of the situation and the risk of collision'*. And although this is a horribly boring bureaucratic piece of text, what it effectively means is that one person cannot be on watch for 24 hours straight, as mental and physical fatigue sets in and keeping a good look-out to prevent collision with other vessels becomes impossible.

But bureaucracy and legal stipulations aside, it is also nice to spread out the workload on the boat between everyone on it, so that you don't clean, cook, navigate and steer all by yourself while someone is lounging away in his or her cabin doing one of the things in the list of What-To-Do-Instead-Of-Tidal-Calculations.

There are many ways of setting up a good rota schedule, and naturally you will have to take in to consideration different factors, such as the duration of the trip, the amount of crew, forecast, your crews' abilities and so on. But regardless of how you do it, and regardless of the different hours of watch, you will eventually end up experience the following chunks in one way or another.

17:00 – 20:00 Sundowner watch

This watch can be quite pleasant for everyone on the vessel. It includes the magic of the sunset, which is naturally accompanied by the social pleasantries of the crew gathering for a lovely Sundowner. Depending on where in the world you are cruising, these are also the hours when dolphins might come out to play for a bit, which obviously provides great entertainment. Finally, it is in these hours that dinner is consumed, and any meal on a boat is an event to look forward to. Well, perhaps not so much for the poor sod in the galley who's slaving away and cooking for the entire crew, thus missing out on both the sunset and the dolphins. Not to mention having to do the washing up afterwards as well.

20:00 – 23:00 Food-coma shift

These hours are particularly great if you happen to be off-watch, as you can put your head down for a few hours and get a nice after-dinner snooze to compensate for the food-coma setting in. It is not so pleasant for the poor sod in the galley who's been slaving away, missing both sunset and dolphins, and who now has to stay awake for a few hours while battling with led-weight eyelids. A few litres of coffee is well needed here.

23:00 – 02:00 Contemplation hour

This shift can be particularly interesting, as one slips into a mental state of personal insights, creative thoughts and just random weirdness roaming around the inside of one's head. This is the pleasant shift where your brain is acting as if it were on some highly illegal drugs, providing you with mental entertainment worthy of the finest visionaries, the most creative minds, or just the most far-out thinkers that should really be locked up somewhere. Luckily you are, technically speaking, locked up on the boat with a bunch of equally crazy people on board.

02:00 – 05:00 Graveyard shift

It's cold, it's dark and it's bloody uncomfortable. You'd much rather be in your bunk, wrapped tightly in your sleeping bag, or possibly in a nice and comfortable hotel room. Minutes drag on, hours feel like lifetimes, and you are so bored that you could easily burst out in a quite embarrassing sulking and sobbing session. Skipper Swede is getting the shivers just by thinking about this quite horrible shift. There is nothing nice to be said about these hours.

05:00 – 07:00 Dolphin hour

There are few things so serene as a sunrise at sea. As you cruise along in the darkness of the night, you gradually become aware of the increasing lightness of the sky above you. The dark celestial dome starts fading away, to be replaced by grades of blue, and the horizon begins to light up as the sun approaches from beneath the world. And then, suddenly, the ball of fire pops up like a cork where sea meets sky, and daybreak enters with a silent explosion of colour, light and magic. This are also the hours when our fat, slippery and playful friends like to come out and put on a show of extraordinary aquatic talent, jumping out of the waves next to the boat, and challenging each other to light-hearted and mischievous games up at the bow. I was once lucky enough to experience a pod of 15 individuals, just in front of the boat, in a straight line perpendicular to our heading, doing synchronized jumping for about half an hour. An amazing sight and indescribable encounter. I promptly named the shift 'The Dolphin Hour' as a homage to these fantastic comrades of the ocean.

Nautical terms, lesson 8

Anchor:

1. Geological instrument designed to at awkward moments retrieve samples of the seabed for later examination.

2. Device that connects vessel with seafloor after five thousand fucking attempts.

3. Metal item rusting away in the bottom of a locker on any given race boat.

Anchor Light
A tiny anchor, or an anchor without flukes.

On Weather

It is quite well known outside of the yachting world that weather forecasts are just as accurate as guessing the upcoming lottery numbers. How many times have you sat in front of your television, eagerly watching the news leading up to the weather forecast for the sake of planning the wonderful trip to the beach the following day. And how many times, the following day, did you arrive to the beautiful beach, covered in sticky suntan lotion, a cool-box filled to-the-brink with beer in one hand, bathing towel size of a small country in the other, just to manage to get rained upon? Blasted weather-man!

Of course this is quite an exaggeration, but I am sure that you, dear reader, will agree that there are more times than what would be considered appropriate where Mr Weather-Man's forecast is complete and utter rubbish.

Quite naturally, this is also the case for the marine forecast. There are more times than there should be when the marine weather forecast is horrendously off. The difference is that when you are on the water, you might find yourself in much more of a dire strait when the forecast is incorrect, than when just heading down to the beach for some sun-bathing and beer-drinking.

There is this particular weather organisation in a country I won't mention, and these amateurs are so far off the mark with their predictions that they might just have forecasted the weather for another continent, on another planet, in a different universe. These guys are so utterly useless at their job that during my 3 months of stay in the country, they didn't manage to get it right even once. Not once! For a good 90 days! A person locked up in a cave, a thousand meters underground, would be more apt at getting the forecast right. Hell, even by guessing randomly one should be able to get the weather right at least once. But not this particular weather organisation, and they were so bad at what they did that I was actually impressed that anyone could be so wonderfully incompetent. It came to the point where I got so fed up and jokingly told my guests that being a weather-man is probably the only profession in the world where you can be wrong all the time and still keep your job.

So for the purpose of this book being not only a collection of Skipper Swedes biased observations and obnoxious thoughts on the yachting industry, but also to provide some kind of useful information, I have the following suggestion for all my fellow sailors: Always use at least 3 different sources of weather forecast. In essence, they are all getting the information from the same supplies such as weather stations, wind meters, barometric pressure readings, satellite images, water temperature and so on. All of the forecasting agencies will then take this information, and based on their own algorithms and calculation methods they will provide the merry sailor with an utterly inaccurate forecast. Hence, when the merry sailor views more than three different forecasts, the sailor can him- or herself build an opinion of the upcoming weather, making the sailor even merrier and more confused than before.

So that is my little suggestion that I hope will help you out in your future yachting adventures, but even when using the forecast of a hundred different weather organisations, the outcome can be laughably wrong. Therefore I'd like to finish this section with this little short extract from the conversation between an instructor and a student, taking place during a class in marine meteorology:

An hour into the class, having gone through everything from global weather patterns to the micro-climate of the sea-breeze, one of the student raises his arm for a question.
"So, what's the weather forecast for today then, sir?"
The instructor relieves a huge sigh and points forcefully towards the window and the scenery beyond it.
"Look out the bloody window! That's the best forecast you will get!"

On Maintenance

There are always jobs to be done on a boat. One of the unwavering facts of boating is that gear will break, parts need to be replaced and maintenance has to be constantly kept on top on. This applies especially to a boat that has a commercial purpose, such as a charter boat, a privately owned yacht, or even a school-boat. This is simply because boats with such a purpose are under much more stress from substantial mileage, wear and tear on the equipment, horrible charter guests flushing down tampons and other nasty things through the maceration pump in the heads, stuffy and arrogant owners who believe they are masters in sailing just because they in fact own the boat you are working on, or plain stupid sailing students who are lacking in the department of basic seamanship, and sometimes also in the mental faculties.

The whole trick of keeping up with maintenance, is that of the prepared sailor who will be on the forefront of perpetual inspection, part replacement and job delegation. Any good skipper who wants to have a neat, tidy and fully operational vessel would make sure that the boat is cleaned thoroughly according to an ongoing schedule, that critical installations such as engine, rigging and electronics are inspected on a regular basis, and that everyone on the ship takes part in the upkeep with enthusiasm and pride.

However, we are all lazy buggers, so there is one fine excuse to use whenever a job presents itself. Enjoy!

On a Mediterranean crossing, every job you could have done, every job you didn't have time to do, every job you didn't feel like doing, every job that you delegated to some inferior crew mate but that was forgotten (or ignored because you were too full of yourself), and every single job that was for one reason or another, unattended, will fall under the following premise:

"It can always be done in Dubrovnik"

This applies for a Mediterranean crossing from West to East, or by all accounts from East to West. Come to think of it, it probably applies for an Atlantic crossing too. Hell, even when circumnavigating the globe, everything can always be left to be done in Dubrovnik.

Regardless of where in the world you are, and where in the world you are heading, you can always wait with the job and do it in Dubrovnik. Simple as that.

On Marinas

Marinas. Harbours. Ports. Wonderful, magic and fantastic places. There are few things as enjoyable as taking a stroll in a marina on a beautiful summers day, cruising easily between the floating pontoons and jetties, listening to the halyards lightly slapping against the masts, and soaking up the beauty of the vessels berthed there.

A marina is a social place, a place where you meet new and old friends, a place where stories are shared, a place of joy, laughter and adventure. There is potential and possibilities in a marina and, if you are open to it, you never know what amazing things might happen, or which horizon life will whisk you away to.

Skipper Swede has spent a great part of his life in marinas. When growing up, a lot of time was spent in my local marina since I was racing and competing heavily. All my friends were there, and it was the natural gathering place for us. We got to work as instructors for younger children, and also as crew on large sailing events. We had a lot of fun, and it's difficult not to look back on those days with my heart filled with nostalgic bliss. As I became older, I also got to visit many new marinas all over the world. Working for a charter company in Australia allowed me to visit some marinas 'down under', and when living in the Caribbean I hopped between islands and got to experience the diversity there as well. And naturally, on all my races around Sweden I got to see some superbly magnificent marinas, although the warmth and weather had much to be desired for. A good friend of mine invited me on a Mediterranean crossing, and for several months we cruised from Gibraltar all the way over to Greece, stopping everywhere we wanted, sightseeing, being tourists and overall having a fantastic trip. So of course, I had the fortune to go to an abundance of marinas on that voyage as well.

However, in some cases, that fortune seemed to be remarkably absent.

One of the reasons why Skipper Swede has been blabbering away about his love and passion for marinas, is simply because a marina can be a truly wonderful place. There is a specific atmosphere and excitement in a marina which cannot be found anywhere else. A marina can be a sanctuary, a world of its own, separated from the hustle and grindstone every-day ordinary world. And even if one doesn't have the same romantic view of a marina as Skipper Swede does, one would have to agree that a marina is still an organisation, and certain services and functionalities will apply to that type of organisation.

But some marinas fail miserably at understanding basic concepts.

One of the things that buggers me is the attitude of people in some marinas. Take, for example, the Caribbean. A lot of the marinas I visited were not particularly developed, and in some cases consisted only of a beach where you had to anchor off and still pay your mooring fees. However, most people had a reasonably nice, friendly and helpful attitude to the yachties, who themselves could often be quite arrogant. The fuel guy would be chatting away in his totally incomprehensible Jamaican/Papiamento/Creole -version of English which left you standing like a deer in headlights, but he still did it with a smile on his face and with the intention to assist you to the best of his ability. The ladies and the port police in some particular harbours would sometimes have a bit of a snotty attitude and practise their position of power-play, but if you knew how to play the game and greet them with respect, politeness and charm you would have your boat papers done faster than you could say "Ja man! Bless!"

But then you arrive to some obscure port in southern Italy after a long crossing, bad weather and little sleep. It's 9 in the morning, and the only thing you want is to park your boat, have a shower and enjoy your obligatory Comealongsider.

There's no one there.

So you wander around the reasonably small marina for a while, finding the harbour masters' office which is obviously closed, and the shower- and toilet block which is not only closed but requires special tokens to be operated. So you'll just have to have another non-luxurious shower on the boat, provided there is enough water left in the tank after your trip. So you go back to the boat, starting to clean up after your journey, undressing and preparing yourself to have that shower. Then you hear some shouting going on from the dock.

It's the harbour master, or at least so you gather after trying to decipher what the little Italian man is yelling at you from the quayside. He is angrily gesticulating and waving his arms around like a small and aggravated windmill, whilst spitting out a torrent of words that certainly doesn't sound like he's praising you. You are too tired, you smell like a crossing, and it is way too early in the morning to be greeted to a new harbour in this fashion.

Turns out after twenty minutes of shouting, that he just wanted the boat to move and park on another dock. Nothing more dramatic than that.

Now, this is a good example of how people in some marinas have no comprehension of how to behave towards their customers, and at the end of the day that is exactly what a yacht and its crew is. Technically, a yacht and its crew are not merely guests in a marina. If they were, they wouldn't be paying for themselves but rather be offered to stay and use the facilities for free. But as this is not the case, the yacht and its crew should then be regarded as paying customers, and that requires a certain approach from the establishment. Friendliness, hospitality and helpfulness are some of the words that spring to mind. Not saying that the customer is always right, but you certainly don't feel like being a good shopper when you are being treated like someone trespassing.

And as someone paying for a service or product you would expect to get some value for your money. I once arrived to a port in Ibiza, and despite the fact that it was off-season, the marina still wanted to charge a horrendous price for our stay. The crew managed to bargain us a better deal, which was still more than three times the daily price for any other reasonably expensive marina in the Mediterranean. But we were welcome to use the toilet and shower block during our stay.

Wonderful.

The toilets had most likely not been cleaned since last season, and the shower cubicles were facing the main entrance and didn't have a door or a curtain, so any passer-by in the street could see you soaping yourself down in all your naked glory. One of the stalls also offered the remains of some dock-workers old lunch that he had failed to put in a rubbish bin.

Yet another non-luxurious shower on the boat then.

So you sometimes wonder what it is you are actually paying for when you visit a marina. If it's not the friendliness or helpfulness, and it's not the shower- and toilet facilities, perhaps it's the water, shore power and Wi-Fi? Nope, not that either, because there are more marinas than I can count where water and shore power is regarded as extras and will add onto your final bill. And when it comes to Wi-Fi, it is quite embarrassing for a marina, in this day and age, not to offer free Wi-Fi. And by all means, if you have to be greedy bastards and charge for such a technological marvel, the Wi-Fi should at least have an internet connection a bit more impressive than an old 28.8 modem.

Now, some places do not offer anything more than the actual dock where your boat is birthed. As mentioned before, several places in the Caribbean are like this, and this is also the case for plenty of marinas in Greece. You will struggle to get any shore power, any water, any fuel, and you will definitely not find any showers, toilets or laundry. However, this doesn't have to be a problem, as you are already aware of the set-up of the marina. Besides, since the cost for staying is very affordable and reflects what you actually get, namely a place for your boat on the dock, you don't really make a big fuzz about it. And even in such a low-cost low-service place, you are still often greeted in a welcoming fashion.

Especially in Greece, the port police are normally very friendly and helpful and will really go out of their way to assist you in whatever way they can. I cannot tell you how many times I've been getting a ride back down to the harbour on the back of Mr Port Police's scooter, one hand holding the boat papers, the other desperately holding on to whatever I can as the guy is happily driving way too fast through the narrow town streets with oncoming traffic, old women crossing the road and the occasional goat enjoying the breeze of us swishing past. But he did offer the ride and that is a service and a gesture not to be ignored.

Most of them are happy for the business, as they realise that your stay is good for the economy of the whole town, and they do take pride in their home and their harbour. However, there is always the rotten apple, and I had the misfortune to take a bite of it whilst working as a flotilla skipper somewhere in the Saronic Gulf.

The lead boat had arrived to this particular port at two in the afternoon, and the rest of the fleet were not too far behind. There were very few mooring points on the dock, as most of the rings had been torn off and the bollards were far apart. But with some ingenuity we still managed to park up a total of 7 boats. At five-thirty, several hours after we had arrived and were all safely tied up to the dock, the port police came down and started barking that we had to move the boats since there was one mega-yacht coming in at seven. I looked at him in disbelief, then at the rest of this dock in the same disbelief, as it offered about 40 meters worth of free space for the singular stink-pot to park.

Obviously, this corrupt pig was getting some serious back-handers that day.

It doesn't exactly encourage you to come back, or to recommend the place to other sailors, does it now? Quite frankly, it sometimes feels that the port police and harbour masters are more like parking attendants than the maître d of the given port. And that's not a particularly flattering comparison for the authoritative organisation of the place.

As said earlier; a marina can be a wonderful, magic, marvellous place with fantastic atmosphere, great people and an abundance of pleasantries. But that also relies heavily on the people running the show and how they approach their clients. So to the benefit of any harbour master, marina owner or port police who might read this, here's a run-down of what a marina should offer to be able to call itself a marina and not, for arguments sake, a shithole:

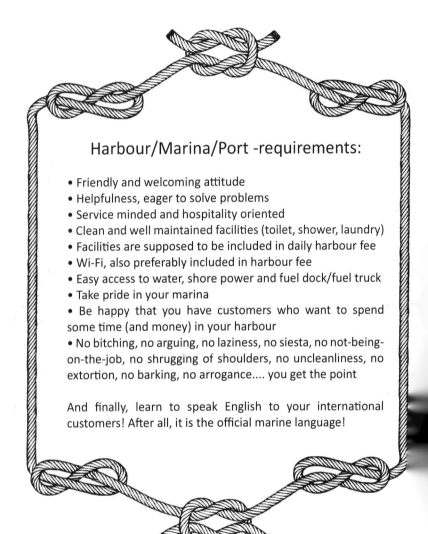

Harbour/Marina/Port -requirements:

• Friendly and welcoming attitude
• Helpfulness, eager to solve problems
• Service minded and hospitality oriented
• Clean and well maintained facilities (toilet, shower, laundry)
• Facilities are supposed to be included in daily harbour fee
• Wi-Fi, also preferably included in harbour fee
• Easy access to water, shore power and fuel dock/fuel truck
• Take pride in your marina
• Be happy that you have customers who want to spend some time (and money) in your harbour
• No bitching, no arguing, no laziness, no siesta, no not-being-on-the-job, no shrugging of shoulders, no uncleanliness, no extortion, no barking, no arrogance.... you get the point

And finally, learn to speak English to your international customers! After all, it is the official marine language!

On Coastguards

Coastguards. Coppers at sea. The term itself sounds quite awesome, and the fine men and women working in this profession normally deserves all credit they can get. These are the people you call when there is trouble afloat, these are the people who make sure that we are safe on the water, these are the people who constantly fight the war on drug smuggling, human trafficking, boat theft, and who patrol the nation's coastline for our protection.

One can almost hear the 70's police series theme music playing. Big moustaches and aviators. Bow-chicka-bow-wow.

The profession itself comes with a quite substantial package of various attributes, whereas the more noticeable are authority and respect. This is the law and order on the water, the sheriffs of the sea and the officers of the ocean. They are upholding the regulations, and in a sense you are expected to do what you are told, because they are performing an important job that keeps us law abiding mariners safe, secure and out of harm's way.

A very good example of this happened as the crew and I were leaving Italy on a particular trip. I had the 'Dolphin-hour' watch, and was happily enjoying the morning coming alive. On the radar I had observed a blip that only popped in to existence every 5 minutes or so, and had apparently done so for the better part of the night and therefore annoyed the crap out of the rest of the crew. I wasn't too bothered, but when the blip suddenly appeared only a few miles away, I pulled out my binoculars and had a look in the appropriate direction. To my surprise, there was quite a large vessel, the size of a very big fishing boat, heading my way. "Poor radar signature for a fishing-boat," I thought to myself and was about to go back to my seat when I saw the rooster tail of a speedboat screaming past me, about half a mile away. Not having seen it until then made me a bit disappointed of my own watch- and lookout skills, but the fact that it didn't show at all on the radar, the fact that it was pushing 30 knots or more, and the fact that my big friendly fishing boat also passed us shortly afterwards, and turned out not to be a big friendly fishing boat, but rather a big scary-ass minesweeping military vessel, made me quite pleased with my deduction that it was the coastguard out chasing a drug runner.

My shift was then about to come to an end, so I headed down below to write an entry in the log. As I was sitting there, I gradually became aware of a very bright light in the saloon. This puzzled me. It was still early morning outside, and no major lights were on down below as the rest of the crew were in their bunks. Yet I could clearly see my shadow displayed on the bulkhead wall. I turned around.

Now, imagine that you look out the companionway only to find yourself staring into the eyes of a huge, menacing-looking, dark-painted monster of a boat hovering just a couple of meters behind your stern, with two spotlights worthy of the Batman signal pointing down your hatch and half a dozen men on the bow with automatic rifles on the ready. Such a sight is an almost magical catalyst for developing superhuman mobility skills for instant teleportation to the bathroom, awkwardly enough at a moment when it would seem very suspicious to run away. Coastguards all over the world have surely had the pleasure of watching sailors perform a fidgety and epileptic version of an Irish Riverdance upon their arrival.

Our whole crew mustered on deck and our skipper got involved in a very polite conversation with the coastguard captain over the VHF. We never got a full explanation, but reading between the lines it seemed that we were being suspected of acting as the mule or 'drop-off-boat' to the little speedboat they had been chasing. After we were cleared of this suspicion, the coastguard drove off in a dramatic cloud of diesel fumes, heading into the sunrise to prevent further crimes and put more bad guys in the slammer.

Bow-chicka-bow-wow.

There is a specific land-lubbers police force that has the wonderful motto 'To Serve and Protect', and that is precisely what the coastguard is there to do as well. These women and men are heroes in their own right and they will do what the motto states, which we tend to forget to appreciate, at least until the excrement are about to hit the shattering device.

One such time for Skipper Swede and his crew was outside of Albania.

The three of us were caught in some reasonably uncomfortable weather; nothing sinister, but enough for us to start considering a secondary destination in case things got worse. After calling up the Albanian coastguard, we not only received several weather updates over the radio from them, but they also called us up every half hour to ask if we needed assistance and to make sure that we were OK.

Needless to say, I was thoroughly impressed by their concern and willingness to help, and the coastguard of Albania has my sincere gratitude and respect after this event. However, this amazing display of support does not exactly happen everywhere, and unfortunately coastguards might just be as stupid, corrupt and anal retentive as any other governmental organisation.

During the third day of a training week, I had the opportunity to initiate my very first Securité-message. The day before, my three students and I had been through a very unexpected thunderstorm. It had come out of nowhere, without any forecast, and caused quite some havoc in the area as we heard everything from holiday cruisers in reasonable distress over the VHF, to stories of structures on land being blown around. Naturally, this was a scary episode for my two Day Skippers and the single guy going for Competent Crew, but they handled it gallantly and were, in retrospect, all very happy to have experienced such an event with an instructor on board instead of being out on the water by themselves wearing brown pants.

The day after, we did several exercises as per the curriculum, and sometime before four in the afternoon, I thought it good to start heading to our destination. Enroute, I spotted a big black chunk of something floating around, about a mile off course. We were all very intrigued and decided to make a quick detour to see what it was. It looked like a capsized fishing boat, or possibly a very large overturned rowing boat, but as we approached it became clear that it was something entirely different. The object was a huge elongated metal cylinder with conical ends, almost like a cigar in shape and approximately 5 meters long and 2 meters in diameter.

For a romantic mariner, it looked remarkably much like the little brother of *Nautilus*. For any other sane person, it looked remarkably military with its heavy metal plating, faded grey paint and conspicuous shape. The name 'Marty the Mischievous Mine' presented itself very quickly.

However, we quickly realised that the object in question must have torn free during yesterday's storm. And being such a clever instructor, I found it to be an opportune moment to discuss various VHF messages and the importance of them. Here we had a big metal object of unknown origin, possibly military, which was clearly visible from afar in the current calm conditions, but imagine if it was dark or if the weather was bad? It could be extremely difficult to spot before it was too late, and could lead to catastrophic outcomes. So a warning had to be issued, and it was not without a staggering amount of pride that I called up Olympia Radio and initiated my first live Securité by reporting our find.

This turned out to be quite a process in itself as I was transferred between different departments through VHF channels and phone calls, but they were superbly friendly and helpful and the message finally came through to the right individual. We were then asked to stay on site for about half an hour, as they would dispatch the nearest Port Police officer to investigate further. And moments later, the Securité was broadcasted on channel 16, complete with Skipper Swede's description of the object, latitude and longitude and prompting it to be an exclusion zone.

I beamed like the lighthouse of Alexandria.

So as requested, we waited. For half an hour. There was still no sign of the dispatched Port Police, and we continuously scanned the horizon and harbours nearby. A few sailboats altered their course to have a quick look themselves of the 'mine', but never came closer than a few hundred meters. Forty minutes later, I called up Olympia Radio again and asked politely where the damn Port Police were at. "He's on his way, Captain, please wait another 20 minutes" came the answer. Right then. How difficult can it be to drive a bloody speedboat 4 miles from here? And why do we need to sit here anyway?

Half an hour after my second call, I called up again and said that we were leaving. I was prompted to stay for another ten minutes as the Port Police was indeed already enroute. As they hung up, the VHF chatter started with some serious exchange of words between Olympia Radio and a vessel, most of the sentences involving several renderings of the Greek word 'Malaka'. They were obviously not happy with each other. But suddenly we saw a speedboat approaching, and the crew and I became very excited to see a conclusion to the quite stimulating afternoon.

It wasn't a coast guard rib that approached. It was instead a red taxi-boat. The Port Police officer was standing with one leg up on the rail and hanging on to the enclosed cockpit with one hand, whilst leaning out so much over the side that he would instantly go in the drink if he lost his grip. This posture made him undoubtedly feel very important and above all, extremely cool. However, he looked like a complete jackass. On top of it, he was wearing aviators.

Bow-chicka-bow-wow.

The students and I did our best not to burst out laughing from the formidable sight of the Greek version of Village People arriving by taxi-boat. I placed myself on the bow for easy communication with the officer, whilst hoping that it was going to be too far away for him to see me smirking. The taxi-boat driver manoeuvred his craft perfectly, slowing down about half a cable-length away so not to create any unnecessary wake on the otherwise flat sea. There was virtually no wind either and it would be easy to hear each other, so he crept up a good 15 meters away from us. The Port Police officer, still in his utterly ridiculous pose, scrutinized our vessel as the taxi-boat came to a halt, then he shouted:
"Hello. You are the Captain?"
"Yes, I'm the Captain," I responded matter-of-factly.
"You call Olympia Radio?" he demanded.
"Yes, that was me," I said.
He went quiet for a second, exchanged a few words with the driver, and then asked, "So what is the problem?"
"Erm?" I gurgled.

I could not believe what I had just heard. Not only had this idiot not been briefed by the authorities about the hazard, he obviously couldn't work out an obvious situation himself either, even when it was right under his nose. Forty meters away, in the completely still and mirror-like sea, was the big black chunk of metal cylinder bobbing around like a happy duck. It wasn't like it could hide anywhere. And this imbecile was asking what the problem was. I was so surprised by his retarded question that I just pointed to the unidentified floating object and said bluntly, "THAT is the problem."

This did not have the intended effect, as he simply proceeded with an even better question, proving once and for all that Sherlock Holmes was indeed Greek. "What is it?" he asked, as if I was the oracle of Delphi and the Sphinx combined.

Well, at least I wasn't smirking anymore.

The conversation went on for a few more minutes with similarly useless questions from the gentleman with a sidearm, until I grew tired and managed to convince him to call his superior, or at least Olympia Radio, to get some clarity himself in the situation. As any other officer of the law, he wouldn't listen to reason or logic from someone inferior, i.e. the public that he serves, but when he realised that he looked like the idiot he was, standing around not knowing what he was looking at, who we were, why he was there or what to do next, he finally picked up his phone and made the call. The driver was then ordered to do a few slow laps around the object, and then he came back to us.

"OK, you can go!" he barked.

"Thank you sir," I replied but was damned if I was just going to take off so easily and continued, "So did they say what it was?"

"Yes, yes, go, go!" he said annoyed and waved us away.

"Ah, good, so what was it then?"

"Yes, go now!" he waved again. Possibly a bit more energetic this time.

"Was it a mine or something else? What did Olympia Radio say?"

"Yes-yes, go now!" he said again.

"What's going to happen with it? Are you towing it away?" I said.

"Go!" he exclaimed, a bit more furiously than before and quickly ordered the driver to start heading away from the annoying Malaka on the sailboat, who stood there smirking at him.

It's not easy to be cool, my friend, when you are an idiot.

Luckily I played that situation quite well, but not always is the outcome from dealing with these inept and defective individuals so easy. On a particular island in the Caribbean, it is said that the coastguard cannot even swim. Whether this is true or not is up for debate, but the very thought of that kind of incompetence for an officer of the ocean is quite terrifying. I've personally had several dealings with said coastguard in the Caribbean, and my sincere and humble opinion is that most of them are complete wankers. Rarely have I come across people who are so staggeringly dumb, and the only thing they have going for themselves is that they can get away with everything thanks to their level of authority and legally justified tyranny. If you are even the slightest bit uncooperative, cocky, or even just want to lighten up the situation by a joke and a smile, you can count on getting boarded, thrown in a very unpleasant Caribbean prison, or shot. Not necessarily in that order.

I could cite numerous stories of my encounters with these imbeciles, but I rather retell one that happened to a good friend of mine: His daughter had just flown over from the UK for a visit and a nice holiday, and my friend had taken her out on his small sailing boat for a cruise around the island and for some recreational diving at a great spot with a sunken wreck. They had moored up and were preparing the diving gear when the coastguard showed up and literally boarded the boat. Not only does it feel horrible to be treated like a criminal and not being able to do anything against the militant force intruding in your life, but also to have to polish off black skid marks from boots and put everything back in order after the prophetical search down below. However, my friend is a cheeky bastard with a quick tongue, and he could probably have avoided a lot of trouble if he would just have kept his gob shut.

As him and his daughter were already dressed up in wet-suits and in the process of setting up the dive tanks, the coastguard pulled up alongside in their over-powered rib. One of them arrogantly demanded: "What are you doing here?" upon which my friend made the hilarious but somewhat unnecessary reply:
"What does it look like we are doing? We are going skiing!"

Instant boarding of vessel...

The successful sailors' attitude:

If you don't know what to say,
If you don't know what has been said,
If you don't know what is being said,

If you don't have the answer,
If you don't know the solution,
If you don't know you were supposed to know,

If you don't know the person talking to you,
If you don't know where you are,
If you don't know who you are,

If shit is about to happen,
has already happened,
or about to go through the fan,
Just say:

"Job's a good-uhn! Uhrrr!!!" * **

*Has to be said in a Cornish accent
**By saying this, it will remove any doubt about your competence

On the Megayacht industry

The only lovely little thing I have to say to most people from this industry that I've had the extensive and intense misery to meet, is that all of you 21-year old, arrogant, naïve, super egocentric, wannabe-celebrity, big spender, San Tropez-and-St Barths –junkie, previously burger-flipping fuckheads, and all of you mid-age, pompous, unfriendly, unhelpful, undereducated, think-you-are-McGuyver crackerjack -deckies with your walkie-talkies shoved right up your arse, and the rest of the morbidly pretentious yet amazingly half-witted and sluggish retards with a perplexing, conceited, up-your-own-alley -high and mighty self-image, that seem to flood this otherwise presumably luxurious industry:

Go fuck yourselves!

You are all a bunch of glorified bus drivers, brownnosing stainless steel polishers and tiller-sucking toilet cleaners. A bunch of empty barrels and rotten windbags. There is no purpose for your existence, and you have no business being on the water.

Nautical terms, lesson 9

Draught or Draft
Something you will be increasingly limited by when around a bar.

Cardinal Marker
A buoy indicating danger, usually shallows. Will always be visually located moments after you've gone aground.

Not Under Command
The successful outcome of a divorce.

On Religiousness at sea

It is no big secret that sailors have been an embarrassingly superstitious lot since the first days of seafaring. From believing in anything supernatural that could assist them in the treacherous and unknown territories they navigated through, to carrying holy symbols, performing invocations and praying with unparalleled vigour to the more well-established religions of the world. Back in the days, it even went as far as sailors tattooing a chicken and a pig on each ankle respectively. The idea behind this bodily art was that these particular animals apparently do not enjoy water, and as the feet are the extremities that, might, first enter when one goes in the drink, the imagery on the ankles were to repel the clumsy sailor from death of drowning. You can clearly see the mind-boggling thought process and majestic level of IQ that has preceded this deduction worthy of Holmes himself.

So sailors have for a long time decided to favour hocus pocus and to put logic and reasoning into the trashcan.

For someone who is fully hands-on with the practical side of hydrodynamics, who can adjusts and form a piece of cloth to adhere to the intricate rules of aerodynamics, and who can navigate successfully and with unbelievable accuracy from A to B using nothing more than celestial objects, it is equally awkward that this someone believes in mythological sea monsters, floating islands and nefarious ghost ships, and of course also that this someone trust various deities to save their day when said proficiency in hydrodynamics, aerodynamics and navigation goes tits up.

Naturally religion is a touchy subject, and we are not here to start a debate on spirituality, religion or belief-systems. As a matter of fact, we sailors only need to glance at what is going on in the rest of the world and what happens when landlubbers feel that their mythology has been invaded, ridiculed or confronted. The result is never a pretty one, and few things are so efficient in creating conflict and distance between human beings that could otherwise co-exist in, if not harmony, then at least a well-calculated and polite repudiation.

Therefore, Skipper Swedes has during his various journeys found that there is a rule that shall apply on every boat, ship or other vessel he embarks on. This is the exact proclamation that occurs every time:

"On this vessel we do not talk about 3 things:
We don't talk about Religion,
We don't talk about Politics,
and We don't talk about sports (particularly football)"

It is fine to discuss these conflict-creating and hostility-inducing topics when one is in harbour and well and clear of both the boat and the sea it travels, although the point of such a conversation seems quite infantile and somewhat unsophisticated to Skipper Swede.

However, as mentioned in the beginning of this text, sailors (and landlubbers alike) has been believing in all kinds of fallacy since the beginning of time. Our created fairy-tales have been given quite a bit of power to govern our sensibility and mental aptness. And naturally, this is also the case for Skipper Swede. However, Skipper Swede choose to believe that if there is some form of a higher power, which Skipper Swede might or might not believe in, it must have a sense of humour. Everything else would be preposterous, illogical and actually morbidly funny in itself. So if this higher power is listening to you when you are out on a boat, you might just as well give the deity a bit of banter. But since one must always be respectful to avoid getting zapped by a well-aimed lightning bolt, you should consider choosing your words with reverence. The following was uttered after a week of being soaked to the bones in a particularly chilly area of the world:

"The Lord giveth,
and the Lord taketh.

So the Lord can bloody well taketh
the fucking rain awayeth."

All of us on the boat were under the impression that the big guy (or girl) upstairs had a good chuckle, as the rain stopped by divine intervention the following day, which strangely enough coincided with the prediction made by the totally unreliable and incompetent weather-man.

Nautical terms, lesson 10

Port:

1. Left on a boat.

2. A place from you wish you never left on a boat.

3. A splendid beverage that there's never any left of on a boat

A Woman in Every Harbour
The true story

There is a rumour that accompanies all seafaring men. A rumour that is rooted in the very earliest days of marine endeavours. Men out at sea for weeks, months or even years, experiencing adventures and exotic places. Men who swashbuckle their way through life, who sleep under the stars and who takes delight in the roar of the ocean. Men who are masters of charisma, who can induce fiery temptation in a woman's heart, and who can sweep anyone they desire off their feet.

There is a rumour that says that sailors – adventurous, dangerous, romantic and devastatingly charming as they are – has a woman waiting for them in every harbour.

This is, to somewhat of Skipper Swede's disappointment, simply not true.

Not even by far.

Nautical terms, lesson 11

Displacement
The reason behind the famous phrase "Why is the rum always gone?!"

Bilge
The other reason, in combination with insecure stowing, behind the famous phrase "Why is the rum always gone?!"

Crew
The third reason behind the famous phrase "Why is the rum always gone?!" Normally follwed by the procedure of keel-hauling of crewmember in question.

A Drink in Every Harbour
The true story

There is a rumour that accompanies all seafaring men. A rumour that is rooted in the very earliest days of marine endeavours. Men out at sea for weeks, months or even years, experiencing adventures and exotic places. Men who swashbuckle their way through life, who sleep under the stars and who takes delight in the roar of the ocean. Men who are masters of charisma, who will enjoy laughter and banter in the company of good friends, and who can sweep every drink off the counter in any given taverna.

There is a rumour that says that sailors – adventurous, dangerous, romantic and likeable merrymakers as they are – will enjoy an abundance of drinks in every harbour.

This is, probably because of the inaccuracy of the other rumour, terrifyingly true.

The liver is not pleased.

Bingeing the compass
32 drinks around the rose

There is a fine practise a sailor can do when becoming superbly bored at sea, known as "boxing the compass". A quick run-down for the uninitiated, boxing the compass is simply the action of naming all the thirty-two points of the compass in correct order, and to do so in a fast succession. Therefore, one would start with "North", and proceed with "North by East", "North-North-East", "North-East by North", "North-East", and so on until all the 32 directions has been covered. The faster one manages to state all the directions, the more entertainment is provided.

One can well imagine the level of boredom that has to occur for such a fun little game to take place.

However, a far more amusing recreation is to drink. There is not a proper sailor in the world that wouldn't agree with this. As a matter of fact, sailors have been drinking since the dawn of seafaring, and this wonderful hobby goes hand in hand with being a sailor. You can neither take the sailor out of the drink, nor the drink out of the sailor. You can always add more drink into the sailor though. And more sailors into the drink, not to forget.

'Semi-functional alcoholics', I believe the term is.

Although drinking is a commendable pastime in itself, Skipper Swede does urgently feel the need to throw in a disclaimer in this little chapter: Obviously we don't commend drinking at sea. It's stupid, ignorant and dangerous. Your ability to react, your proficiency at solving difficult situations, even your authoritative skills as the Master of the Vessel, are all impeded heavily when you drink at sea.

No matter how good you are as a drinker, you will find all your abilities diminishing by the glass, and you are certainly not, despite what you might think at the time, becoming cleverer, funnier or a better singer. So don't drink at sea.

You are more than welcome to get entirely sloshed when arriving to port though.

There is an abundance of pleasant drinks that a sailor can indulge in, and since drinking is such a more pleasant recreation than boxing the compass, Skipper Swede thought that it would be a good idea to have a drink representing each and every direction. That way, you can enjoy this little game by drinking your way through the whole compass circle, and also see who can actually stand up when arriving half-way. You could also have this guide as a reference, so depending on your vessels' direction when entering a new harbour or when moored up, that direction will be the designated drink for the duration of your stay. That becomes even more fun when free-swinging on a mooring or anchor. Be sure to stock up your supplies before.

I sincerely hope that you, my fellow sailor, will enjoy this list of wonderful and palatable drinks. They have been collected by Skipper Swede himself during his many journeys around the world, and has provided much entertainment and joy for both Skipper Swede and the fellow sailors (and occasional land-lubbers) he's had the pleasure to drink with. Perhaps one day you and I might even have one or two, or thirty-two, of these drinks together. Wouldn't that be a ball!

Enjoy responsibly and in royal quantities!

"Any damn fool can navigate the world sober. It takes a really good sailor to do it drunk."

- Sir Francis Chichester

North – Beer

There are few things as enjoyable as a nice cold beer at the end of a day. Or an ice cold beer for that matter (see what I did there?!). It doesn't matter where in the world you are, if the climate is hot or cold, if you are indoors at the cosy Yacht Club or drinking outside in the sunshine, alfresco. A beer is always highly appreciated, and quite often mind-numbingly tasty. And if you are not drinking your favourite beer, at least any beer with a justifiable alcohol content is just as pleasantly mind-numbing on its own.

North by east – Bloody Mary

The most complex of drinks, commonly known as a 'hair-of-the-dog' drink. Because there are no facts supporting the claim of it being a hang-over cure, it was probably invented by alcoholics to validate drinking in the morning, which Skipper Swede thinks is quite a fine practise. There are millions of ways to make a Bloody Mary, and I suggest you do a quick search online for pictures of this drink defying all common sense and logic. How about garnishing with a hamburger, a club sandwich, or even another Bloody Mary? However, as Skipper Swede does immensely enjoy a properly made Bloody Mary, here's his own personal recipe.

    1 part Vodka
    2 parts Tomato Juice
    A bit of salt
    Quite a hefty bit of black pepper
    A good few splashes of Worcestershire sauce
    A good few splashes of hot sauce (Tabasco or even better; Caribbean scotch bonnet pepper hot sauce)
    Ice
    Garnish, only if you're supposed to be artsy-fartsy.

North-northeast – Absolut Salty Dog

This drink will probably not suit more than a handful of any given population in a bar, but the name has a satisfying ring to it, and the taste is remarkably descriptive. The flavours are: Pungent (condition of strong, sharp smell that is often terribly unpleasant), Sour (a state of hostile acidity) and Salty (the state you find yourself in after a day on the water). So having this drink is just like having... erm... a salty ol' seadog. Ahem.

3 parts Absolut® Peppar vodka (yes, it is spelled that way. It's a Swedish vodka, you tosser)
½ part Grapefruit juice
Salted rim on the glass

Northeast by north – (Special) Singapore Sling

The Singapore Sling is a unique and complex drink with lots of history to it. If you can make one with all the ingredients, then you are in for a real treat. However, some stuff might be difficult to get when you are sitting in a marina of what feels to be somewhere on the outskirts of the Dark Ages, so be inventive and make your own 'Special' Singapore Sling with whatever you can get your hands on!

2 parts Gin (it would be embarrassing if you can't find some gin, or already have it on board...)
1 parts Cherry Liqueur or Cherry Brandy (or just cherry juice for flavour)
0.5 parts Cointreau®
0.5 parts Bénédicte® (or a substitute for a sweet herbal liqueur)
1 part Grenadine
8 parts Pineapple juice
1 part lime juice
Dash of Angostura Bitters®

Northeast – Vodka

It would not seem right not to honour our lovely neighbours up in this direction of the world. Swedes do in general love vodka, but arguably the Finns love it just a bit more. Mixed in any drink, or, whilst slapping each other joyfully with birch twigs in your nearest sauna, it can also be enjoyed in its natural form; straight out of the bottle.

Northeast by east – Skipper's Coffee

A variant on the famous and delicious Irish Coffee. However, since skippers are generally as poor as Job's turkey, any spirit will have to do. And since the only coffee found on a boat is nasty instant brown caffeine powder with characteristics vaguely reminiscent of coffee, that will have to do as well. And forget the whipped cream, because it'll only go bad the very moment it's brought onto the boat, so use powdered milk instead. Or rather, don't drink this at all.

East-northeast – Commodore's Coffee

The more exclusive variant of Irish Coffee, usually had by the wankers of all wankers, the Commodores. These arseholes are often self-titled heads of a yacht club, the chiefs of a marina, or the bosses of a charter company, and they are so full of themselves that skippers seem to be the manifestation of selflessness and compassion in comparison. However, the drink is remarkably pleasant.

    1 part Galliano
    1 part dark or golden Rum
    1 part espresso, preferably Illy®
    Whipped cream on top

East by north – The Gale

A surprisingly tasty cocktail with the inspiring colour of either a gorgeous tropical blue lagoon, or antifreeze for your car. And it has an awesome nautical name!

    3 parts Vodka
    1 part Vermouth
    1 part Galliano
    1 part blue Curacao
    Lime juice & Ice

East – Navy Russian

This is pretty much the same as the classic drink 'White Russian', with the only difference that you use Baileys instead of milk. The benefit of doing so is that you get a creamier beverage, which also happens to have a much better alcohol percentage.

    1 part Vodka
    1 part Kahlua®
    2 parts Baileys®
    Serve with a few cubes of ice

East by south – Lonely Island Ice Tea

A variant on the classic Long Island Ice Tea, with the quite unsurprising twist that you take pretty much any white spirit you have left in the liquor cabinet and add it to your glass. Top up with lemon- or lime juice and cola, or whatever else you might have left in the galley. The left-overs of your heavily sugared tea might just do the trick. And why the name? Because it's a shame to leave the bottles all alone in the cupboard. Poor things.

East-southeast – Tipuru, Raki, Grappa

This shit is vile. It is so disgusting that it is almost an insult to the person drinking it. The flavour, if you can call it that, is unbelievable rancid and offensive, and the liquid would serve better purpose as a degreaser of engines or fuel for space travel. That is possibly the reason to why people drink it and why it is, contrary to all sense and logic, quite enjoyed. If Skipper Swede has even half a shotglass of these spirits, please be aware that he cannot be held accountable for anything for the coming 12 hours, and that any form of recollection of events taking place is by definition impossible.

Southeast by east – Rum & Coke

Another terribly simple and common cocktail that is in effect designed to take away the beautiful flavour of your fine rum, or to camouflage the noxious taste of the cheap shit you bought in tax-free. A good drink when you are on-the-go, as components are reasonably easy to come by and the making of the drink takes less than 5 seconds, if you are good. No ingredient description needed, but do consider throwing some lime in the mix.

Southeast - Piña colada

The more colourful and exotic cocktails originating from warmer climates belongs quite naturally to the southern part of the compass. These are the drinks with stupid little umbrellas stuck into various parts of the enormous fruit garden circumferencing the rim of your glass, and the drinks that should preferably not be consumed whilst wearing a Hawaii shirt, a Panama hat, white socks and loafers. You might be mistaken for a relic from the 80's. However, Piña Colada is such a classic, and it deserves an honorary position in this list of drinks. That is why it is the first one of the southern drinks, and although there are as many ways of making it as there are bars and bartenders in the world, here is the rough guideline for its contents.

1 part white Rum (I would suggest more to be honest)
3 parts pineapple juice
1 parts coconut cream (such as Coco Lopez®)
Mix with ice in a blender
Garnish with a pineapple wedge on the glass

Southeast by south – Sea Breeze

A cocktail that happens to be dangerously refreshing and therefore having quite an accurately describing name. As you down several of these without any hesitation or current headache, it will have the poetic effect of a breeze entering one ear and exiting the other, taking your brain with it in the process.

1 part Vodka
3 parts Cranberry Juice
1 part Grapefruit / Pineapple / Blood orange, depending on your level of tropicality.

South-southeast – Bahama Mama

Rum, rum, rum! A proper sailor loves his rum! Then add flavours of coconut, coffee and some tropical pineapple into the mix and you have a classic drink worthy of any exotic tiki-hut on the beach.

½ part Tia Maria®
1 part golden Rum
1 part coconut Rum (such as Malibu®)
1 part dark Rum
3 parts pineapple juice
Lemon juice
Ice

South by east – Dark & Stormy

A harsh and powerful drink sporting a name that invoke thoughts of bad weather, pirate battles, ghost ships and nefarious sea monsters. "Arrr! Avast ye scallywags! Heave ho and there'll be grog!"

    1 part Gosling's® black Rum
    1-2 parts ginger beer
    Slice of lime

South – Painkiller

Painkiller is probably Skipper Swedes favourite rum-based tropical-style cocktail. Originally, the drink came from some beach bar in the US virgin islands, and managed to spread to the rest of the world thanks to its simplicity, wonderful taste, and because it's so dangerously consumable. Skipper Swede's first encounter with this lovely concoction rendered him absolutely incomprehensible and quite embarrassingly stupid, as he devoured the better part of a litre of fine rum in a few hours time on a sunny and hot Caribbean afternoon. A very pleasant experience, the little of it that he can remember.

    2 parts golden Rum (such as Mount Gay®)
    1 part orange juice
    1 part pineapple juice
    0.5 parts or less Coco Lopez®
    Some dashes of nutmeg
    Mix with ice in a blender

South by west – Light & Breezy

This is a drink that Skipper Swede almost invented all by himself, although it's so simple that he can barely take credit for its manifestation, and probably not even its cleverly constructed name. It came about whilst he was visiting his favourite bar in the Caribbean, and he suddenly felt the urgent desire to have a Dark & Stormy. However, the bartender informed him that they didn't have the ingredients necessary to compose one, as they weren't stocked with neither black rum nor ginger beer. So instead, a similar drink was thrown together with regular golden rum and ginger ale, and since it had both a much lighter colouring and a sweeter, more refreshing taste, it became a Light & Breezy! Ta-daaa!

1 part golden Rum (such as Mount Gay®)
1-2 parts ginger ale
Serve with a few cubes of ice

South-southwest – Tingeling

I was on the verge of not putting this drink in here, but it's one of those that is so immensely stupid, whilst actually tasting quite nice, that I didn't have the heart to leave it out. This particular drink has the flavour of an ice lolly (popsicle if you are American or Canadian) and when consumed this set of flavours sends very strange signals to your brain. But then again, who doesn't want to get drunk on something that tastes like an ice cream and has the name of an obscure small-town hooker!

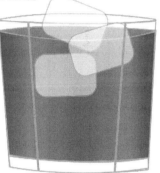

1 part Malibu® coconut rum
1 part Ting® (or equivalent grapefruit soft drink)
Serve with a few cubes of ice

Southwest by south – Dirty Banana

This is a surprisingly tasty drink, which will please most people you serve it to. However, the kicker with this cocktail is the quite suggestive name, which usually brings out a few laughs, and also the serving method as the brown, decomposing banana skin hanging off the side of the jug does not look anything short of disgusting.

1 part golden Rum (such as Mount Gay®)
½ part Kahlua®
1-2 parts milk, or preferably cream
A few fresh bananas
Chocolate syrup
Mix with ice in a blender
Serve in a jug, garnish with the decomposing banana skin hanging off the side

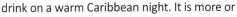

Southwest – Caribbean mudslide

A wonderful and rich drink that is best enjoyed as an after-dinner drink on a warm Caribbean night. It is more or less the same recipe as a normal mudslide, so if it wasn't for the alcohol content, this drink could probably be eaten with a spoon and pass for a chocolate sundae.

1 part golden Rum (such as Mount Gay®)

½ part Kahlua®

2 parts Baileys® (or milk, or a combination)

Splash of Frangelico®

Lots of chocolate syrup

Mix with ice in a blender

Southwest by west – Mojito

Hemingway loved this. If Hemingway loved it, it has to be alright.

Sugar (preferably brown, or sugar cane juice)

Fresh mint (preferably mortared with the sugar)

1 part White rum

0.5 parts Lime juice (squeezed from fresh lime)

3 parts Club soda / Sparkling water

Ice

West-southwest – Port

This fortified wine is a true delight. Produced exclusively in the wonderful land of Portugal, this distilled spirit can be enjoyed at many different occasions. It serves well as a pre- or after dinner drink, as an evening pleasure or nightcap, or even when one is far away from the ocean; while lying in the warm bathtub, longing for the sea and dreaming of days of sailing. The latter has raised quite a few eyebrows when described to land-based cave-dwellers.

West by south – Margarita

There are funny sayings about this drink, and my favourite ones are "When life gives you lemons, grab some tequila and make a Margarita!" and "The only thing better than a Margarita, is two Margaritas". You can't really argue with either! This drink is a treat, whether on the rocks or as a frozen slush. Arriba!

    2 parts Tequila
    1 part Cointreau®
    1 part lime juice
    Ice
    Salted rim on the glass

West – Port and Starboard

We sailors get somewhat like a fat kid in a candy store the moment something nautical-inspired emerges. So although this drink, or shot, is not that particularly spectacular, it has to be added because of the awesome name and presentation alone.

    1 part Grenadine® (red)
    1 part Crème de Menthe® (green)
    Pour carefully so that the crème de menthe floats on grenadine.
    Shout out "Land-ho!" at the moment of consumption.

West by north – Gin & Tonic

An institution amongst sailors and travellers, and doesn't need any further introduction. However, the making of it is a surprisingly detailed art and should be adhered to in order to produce an exclusive yet regular cocktail.

    A few mashed lime wedges in the glass
    A good squeeze of lime juice
    Ice
    1 part gin
    2 parts tonic
    Sugar on the rim, along with lime

West-northwest – Champagne

The fine drink of celebration. The drink of champions and winners. The drink of the exclusives and aristocrats, and those who momentarily want to be like one. Can be enjoyed with elegance at any fine event, and when success has been achieved. However, mix it with orange juice and consume it before 10am and it has suddenly become breakfast and is called a Mimosa.

Northwest by west – Sloshed Sailor

The cocktail 'Drunken Sailor' comes in many shapes and forms, but every variant seems to include two spirits. So therefore, the 'Sloshed Sailor' must naturally have had a bit more to drink and 4 spirits should do the trick and render you perfectly blitzed.

1 part Golden rum
1 part Gin
1 part Vodka (preferably flavoured)
1 part Tequila
Lemon juice, grapefruit juice
Pinch of salt
A few dashes of Angostura Bitter®

Northwest – Tea

Yup, you read that absolutely correct. Tea. That fantastic brew that has invigorated mankind for over 3000 years, without the addition of alcohol (although one could). This is a perfect choice of drink when arriving to port, in the morning, during the day, anytime in the day, on a cold day, on a hot day, and frankly just about any day. One can enjoy a hot brew at any given moment in time. And if my instructors and sailing friends from the UK will ever read this, I'm sure they will be very proud of me. Cheers old chaps!

Northwest by north – Pimms

Besides tea, it doesn't get more British than this. This drink is an institution for the Britts, and it can be seen being devoured in astronomical quantities during summertime, and quite often around boats. It was created in 1823 by a gentleman called James Pimm, and the Pommy tradition has apparently been going on since.

   1 part Pimm's
   2 parts Lemonade (or better: Sparkling white wine)
   Sliced Apple, Lemon, Orange and Cucumber
   Her Majesty the Queen's Royal Accent

North-northwest – Whiskey

Another fine spirit that will often bring delight to a sailor. It will often also bring relaxation, then exaggerated storytelling, then dissonant singing and finally a comatose state of mind known as 'plastered'. One of Skipper Swede's favourites is 'Chivas®'. In case you're in the neighbourhood.

North by west – Martini

This is undoubtedly the most elegant drink on this list, and be sure that you can rise to the occasion and keep the same high standards yourself when you have one. There is a certain air, spectacular class and total finesse with a Martini, and such a drink deserves more than to be consumed by someone wearing sloppy old jeans and a t-shirt with some obnoxious print on it. This is the drink for mingling, the drink at dinner parties, the drink for the casino, a drink Churchill enjoyed, and of course the signature drink of James Bond. And who doesn't want to feel like James Bond once in a while? There are several variants to suit any palette, but the following is the base.

   6 parts Vodka or Gin
   1 part Vermouth
   Suitable garnish (olives, orange peel etc.)
   Dinner jacket, evening dress or similar outfit worn by consumer.

Bonus drinks

Sundowner

Yes, yes, yes, we do not drink at sea. However, there are moments when a sailor will drink to honour tradition. Some of the more known moments are when rounding the Horn or crossing the equator, whereupon the sailor shall toast to a whole bunch of various things, events and supreme beings, including King Poseidon. The Sundowner is a fine tradition to honour the fact that you have been on the water the whole day. Well, maybe you've only been out for a few hours, but the point is that the day, with its sunlight, is over and night is upon you. So you have a drink and toast to the sun setting and a day well spent, doing something you are passionate about and that you love doing. Some good Sundowners include Bloody Mary and Rum & Coke.

Comealongsider

A wonderful drink with a clear purpose. This is your reward after some serious effort out on the water for several weeks, a stormy day, or possibly when you've managed the lengthy journey to and from the fuel pontoon inside the harbour. The Comealongsider, is as its name suggests, a drink to reward you for the hard work, and a drink you shall have when the boat is secure at the dock and you have come alongside. The choice of beverage is quite bloody irrelevant, but plenty of sailors prefer an ice cold beer or a Gin & Tonic, both classifying as excellent choices.

Approacher (a.k.a. Nearlier)

This is the pre-comalongsider drink, and yet another one of those drinks we officially don't have, as it is consumed while still on the water. This drink is had when your trip is almost over and you are approaching the harbour, hence the name "Approacher", or since you are nearly there; "Nearlier". If you want to be a good boy, you could always have the drink from the Northwest. But then again, if you are from the UK you've probably had enough brews during your day of sailing to open up a small Indian trading company all by yourself.

Water

You might think that Skipper Swede has lost all of his marbles by adding water into this list, but that could not be further from the truth. To be able to keep up with the rest of the crews' drinking habits, it is critical that you rehydrate your system in between the sessions. Also, as the disclaimer in the beginning of this chapter stated, it is insanely stupid to be drunk whilst at sea, and the best remedy for it is lots and lots of water. Alcohol is unfortunately a poison, and to be able to enjoy this poison frequently and in imperial quantities, water is the ultimate solution to counterbalance an otherwise very heavy load on your system. Besides, you do not want to say something similar to what a very good friend and fellow skipper revealed to me the day after a reasonably big drinking session:

"I should probably have some water, because my pee did not have the colour of Champagne this morning!"

Nautical terms, lesson 12

Mizzen:

1. The Dinghy.
2. A harbour space
3. Your boat keys
4. Good crew
5. Money
6. Good sailing conditions
7. The Rum.

On breaking out in song

There is a mysterious and haunting phenomenon happening at sea. It is a dreadful spectacle that has been going on for eons. From the tiniest of rowing boats, to the crazy speed-seeking dinghies, from the ocean-crossing circumnavigator, to the island-hopping cruiser, from the most majestic of battleships, to the most humble of home-builds. On any vessel on the oceans, seas and lakes of the world, there is a common occurrence that has no founding in normal logic, or even normal social manners.

On any boat it seems that the merry sailor, or the grumpy captain for that matter, will almost automatically break out in song. This might happen at any given moment, with any given song, and in any given off-key. And usually to the great disturbance and disagreement of anyone around.

Not that opinions of others usually matters in those circumstances.

This phenomenon is quite fascinating and mysterious at the same time. Perhaps it comes from the sense of freedom that encapsulates any seafaring individual. Maybe it originates from a lesser number of criticising ears and the fact that glass that can break is a rare commodity on most boats. Or it could possibly have something to do with the vastness and endlessness of the sea itself, posing as your personal Royal Albert Hall with an enchanted audience of fish, cetaceans, cephalopods, molluscs and the occasional seaweed cheering you on with their subaquatic, and silent, applause.

In either way, a happy boat is a good boat, and to break out in song makes the boat so much more festive, except for the poor suckers who have to listen to the garbage. Personally, Skipper Swede has had the displeasure of listening to many merry sailors who, in disregard to surroundings, decided to break out in song. There was for example this gentleman who the crew and I made good friends with while we sat put in La Linea for a few days during a delivery. He was a great laugh, had a snappy whit and quick tongue, and a master in chucking down beers in the bar. Unfortunately he was also a terribly chirpy morning person, and usually greeted us by elephanting onto the yacht, sticking his head down the companionway and roaring something totally incomprehensible along the lines of 'Morning has broken'.

If it wasn't for his charming persona, the crew would have made sure that the morning would not be the only thing breaking that day.

A great person and good friend that Skipper Swede once worked with had the good taste in music to enjoy the band Queen. He had the lesser good taste in singing it passionately out loud, at random and often at awkward occasions. He also had the quite embarrassing, but nonetheless very charming and absolutely hilarious way of greeting customers, tavern owners, seagulls and the world in general by bawling the initial 3 lines of lyrics to Freddie Mercury's 'It's a beautiful day'. He never made it further, for reasons untold. But we were all very content with only being presented that extract, and nothing more.

Now, since Skipper Swede is in fact a skipper and a sailor as well, it is quite natural that Skipper Swede breaks out in song every now and then too, just as any other mariner. Naturally at the most inappropriate moments, and often with a singing voice so grim that flowers would wither and birds would fall dead out of the trees if they were in close proximity. Nonetheless, a song is there to be sung, and during a few days on a flotilla, the whole fleet found itself blown-in and unable to leave harbour due to some serious winds, thunder and downpour. To amuse the guests, Skipper Swede composed the following masterpiece and performed it with great pride and gusto, which unfortunately only had the effect that he did not see his clients for the rest of the day.

Do try to sing along, dear reader.

Original song: 'Who wants to live forever'
Writer, original piece: Brian May
Producers: Queen, David Richards

There's no sun for us
Only rain for us
What is it with, this bloody wind, that's howling down on us?

Who wants to sail this weather?
Who waaaants to saaaail this weather?
(ooooohh...)

There's no sail for us
There's no freedom for us
We're stuck in here, our crew in fear, this day is a real anus.

Who wants to sail this weather?
Who waaaants to saaaail this weather!?
Noooooooooot me!

(instrumental)

Who dares to sail this weather
(Nooo-uuuh-oh-oh!)
To get drunk will suffice

(Instrumental; Brian May's Star Wars tie-fighter inspired guitar solo)

It's supposed to be, a lovely breeze
Not this ma-aa-adness, with five meter seas

So we won't sail this weather!
Instead, let's drink together!
We'll never go out in this (anyway)

Who wants to sail this weather
Who wants to sail this weather
This weather is not ok
Let's stay in harbour for the day* **

*Feel free to recompose according to your own pleasure and whim, especially with improved description of current weather condition and the overall attitude of the involved crew

**At any given point during the performance of this song, an air-guitar should be ferociously played upon

On blonde moments

We all have them. Those moments when you wish you could sink through the floor. Those moments you wish that you were invisible, in another country, on another planet, or preferably all of it at once. Those moments you hear yourself saying something so remarkably stupid, that you wonder how it is even possible to be that dumb. Those moments when you realise at the same time as your lips are moving, that the horrible things jumping spontaneously out of your mouth like frisky little rabbits are never going to go down well. Those moments when you wonder how you will ever be able to live this down, since you've just made a complete and utter twat out of yourself.

Skipper Swede is definitely no exception. And since I've been quite proficient at bashing other people's stupidity throughout this book, I thought it only fair to reveal some of my own personal face-palm moments. Enjoy!

PS. Skipper Swede's natural hair colour happens to be... that's right. Blonde.

Horrendously blonde moment number 1

This lovely incident took place on a delivery of a Bavaria 46 between Falmouth and Southampton in the UK. It was just before the Southampton boat show in late autumn, and the wonderful UK weather had blessed us with 10 degrees Celsius during the day, overcast, rain, Force 5-7, and waves from three different directions. As that was not enough, we were only two people on the boat, which also lacked in the autopilot and electronic navigational department.

However, I was thrilled and excited as it was my first 'job' with my newly acquired YachtMaster qualification, and I was eager to get hands-on as I was now a recognised and commercially qualified skipper.

I seemed be quite delusional in that aspect.

It's an understatement to say that the trip itself was quite demanding, and it took us a bit over 36 hours to arrive to Southampton. Throughout the journey we got soaked by the rain, sloshed around by the confused sea, sleep deprived as the two of us had to be on watch for an hour only at a time, and mentally exhausted as we only had the compass to steer by. And we steered manually the whole way.

So in the middle of the darkness, sometime around 10 at night, I noticed that the compass light had gone out on the starboard helm. I quickly moved over to the port steering wheel and regained my course, then shouted down to my comrade below:
"Hey buddy, the compass light just went out. Can you check the nav panel?"
"Sure thing," the muffled reply came from down below. A few moments passed. "No, the instruments are switched on. Tell me what happened."
As he was the senior skipper, I wanted to make a good impression and quickly come up with various reasons for the malfunction. "It just went out on Starboard side. Maybe it's the light bulb in the compass," I shouted through the torrential downpour. "Or it could be a fuse somewhere. Possibly even some wiring that got wet with all this rain."

"Hang on, let me check." A few more moments passed and he came up through the companion way. "No, I checked everything and I cannot find any problems. We'll have a closer look in the morning when the sun is up and we can actually see something."

It sounded good to me, and I was about to come off watch anyway. The horrible night proceeded in complete darkness with no stars or moon for orientation, only the port side compass told us where we were heading. Waves were throwing the boat around and intense and constant focus was required to stay within even 30 degrees of our desired course. And sleep was virtually impossible, both due to the violent movements of the boat, and also because as soon as you started to drift into unconsciousness, an hour had already passed and your shift was beginning again.

By early morning, about an hour before sunrise, it calmed down a little and I went down below again and finally managed to fall asleep, with the emphasis on 'fall' or rather 'collapse'. My senior skipper were kind enough to let me sleep longer than the watch and I came up again after a total of nearly two hours. He had a very annoying grin on his face.

"Morning!" he said mischievously.

"Morning," I replied, confused to if the night had gotten the better of him and he had lost all of his marbles. "Do you want a cup of tea?" I asked.

"Sure, but before you do that, do you know what happened with the compass light last night?"

I became intrigued. "Ah, is it working now? Was it the light bulb itself? Or was it something with the wiring?"

His grin spread even wider, a mad Cheshire Cat at the helm. "Nope, but good effort for trying though."

"So what was it?"

"The cover had blown over it".

Aaaaahh!!! Face-palm!!!

Horrendously blonde moment number 2

As already mentioned previously in this book, I had the great fortune to tag along with a friend of mine on a jolly 'ol trip across the Mediterranean. A luxurious and pleasant Beneteau Oceanis 50 was the vessel, and the two of us were the main crew as friends flew out on various legs of the trip to join the adventure. At one point it had attracted a gentleman who had recognised the great opportunity for him to gain some more mileage to add to his upcoming YachtMaster trainings, whilst enjoying a sail in the spectacular Mediterranean waters.

As a matter of fact, there was another benefit as well which attracted him to this particular journey; both my friend and myself were qualified RYA Cruising Instructors. Naturally, he had the intention to pick our brains and leave with as much knowledge and information as possible, which I thought it was a brilliant idea, and I was more than happy to share my expertise with him. Anything to help a fellow aspiring man of the sea.

Notice how I used the words 'man' and 'sea' in that particular order? That's right. That's because Skipper Swede pronounces it 'Bu-ee'.

The sun had just set and the yacht was tugging along under motor as there was little wind this night. The stars were coming out, and we ploughed along steadily through the calm water. Although I had another 20 minutes before my watch, I had joined him up on deck and we were entertaining ourselves with discussing different collision regulations, day signals, sound signals, as well as figuring out the different light shapes around us.

"What is that," I said and pointed towards a set of lights some 8 NM away.
"Let me see," he said and peered towards the structure of lights. "Well, it's probably over 50 meters as it has a those two white lights. And we are seeing it from port side, because of the red light."
"Yes, that is correct, well done. Have a look over there, what do you think that is?" I pointed out towards land where a small vessel was making way.
"Hmm," he said and scratched his head. "Well, we see it from

starboard side because of the green light. And it's motoring."

"That is correct, but what about the other two lights?" I asked him. He was quiet for a spell.

"Nope, really don't know mate" he said and shook his head.

"It's a fishing vessel" I said. "Remember the rhyme to remember it by; 'Red over white, fishing at night'? And since it is the red and white light and not the green and white light, he is doing something other than trawling, for example long-lining, and therefore we should really stay out of his way."

"Right, that's actually a good rhyme," he said with a smile. "Quite stupid, but it makes it easy to remember it by."

I couldn't agree more, and during the next ten minutes I ran through all of the rhymes and memory techniques that I had used myself during my trainings. A few of them are quite silly and we did manage to have a few laughs before he stood up and announced that he would write his entry in the log and leave me to my shift. As he was about to enter the companionway he stopped and looked towards land. He turned to me who was making myself comfortable for my watch and asked "Do you see that light? What is that?"

I looked to where he was pointing and some 5 NM away, a red light was making its way through the night.

"That's interesting," I said. "What would you say it is?"

"Well it's supposedly a sailing vessel seen from its port side, but it's moving way too fast, isn't it?"

"I agree," I said. The vessel was doing at least 20 knots, slowing down and speeding up again. It was hard to tell with only the dark backdrop of the mountains as a reference. "I'd say it's a power vessel with a broken steaming light."

"Yeah, that makes sense," he said. "Well, I'll just write the log and then I'll put my head down."

"Alright, enjoy your kip and see you later tonight!"

I turned back to the erratic red port-side light that seemed to be totally inconsistent in its speed and movements. Although the broken steaming light seemed to be the most logical explanation, I could not shake the feeling that it wasn't the right one. I sat there and stared at it for a good few minutes. It didn't even move the way it should, and even if was a powerboat doing circles and playing around, no-one does that at that time of night.

And then it struck me.

Although I had rather preferred to keep my dignity as a YachtMaster and especially a Cruising Instructor by simply keeping my mouth shut, the obvious answer was so embarrassing and laughable that I could not but to share it with someone. So I jumped over to the companionway and stuck my head down to where my fellow crewman had just finished writing the log entry and was in the process of taking off his wet weather gear.

"Hey buddy," I said. "I realised what that red light was."

"Yeah?" he said. "It wasn't just a broken steaming light?"

"No, it's much worse than that," I said. He looked at me confused.

"It was the tail light of a car on the hills."

Aahhh!!! No, no, no, no, no, you idiot!

Horrendously blonde moment number 3

This one is so hideously awful that I'm almost ashamed to include it in the book. This incident should never, ever, under any circumstances, happen to a reasonably seasoned sailor, especially not to one who is using his YachtMaster certification on a commercial level and therefore actually doing this for a living. To be able to enjoy such a dramatic seizure in mental functions as I did that day, should easily put me on the same cerebral level as a grapefruit.

One lovely day, I was working as a flotilla-skipper together with my hostess. We were motor-sailing to our destination; she was up helming, and I was down on the Nav-station doing some administrative work on my computer. She shouted down to me.
"The wind is picking up, I'll pull the throttle back a bit."
"Sure thing," I responded. Realising that this would affect the power output from the inverter that my computer was connected to, I shouted back "Just pop it out of gear and give it some revs. I need to continue charging my laptop."
"Ok, not a problem," she replied sprightly and did what I asked, and then returned to enthusiastically sailing the yacht through the lovely breeze.

About half an hour later I had finished my work on the computer, and came up to see if she wanted to be relieved. She did indeed and said that even though it was really good sailing, she should have a quick lie-down before we arrived so that she would be rested for the evening with the guests. She promptly went down below, and I took the seat at the helm. The scenery between the islands passed as I kept sailing towards our destination and I took the time, as one does when alone on the helm, to contemplate and meditate. I was very content and felt fortunate with my profession and lifestyle. With the beautiful scenery around me, under the warm sunshine, in a sailing vessel, there was nothing to complain about. I was living the dream, doing what I love to do, and getting paid for it. "Bloody nice day, that's for sure," I mused and rubbed my hands together. "Good sailing too. Although the wind has dropped a bit, and we're only doing 4 knots. Better put some more revs on the engine". Another ten minutes ticked by, and the wind dropped even more. "Must be the lull before the afternoon breeze," I thought to myself. "Let's put some more revs down". Another ten minutes, and the wind had now dropped to only a light Force 3. We were doing around 2.5 knots. I started to get puzzled by the lack of performance in the boat. Both the main and genoa was fully up, and the engine ticking over at 2100rpm. We should be doing more than 2.5 knots. I looked over the transom to see if we had accidentally caught a rope or tarpaulin, or anything else that could slow us down, but there was nothing there. Could the propeller have fallen off? Unlikely, as the sound and feeling in the boat had been the same for hours. And there was no tidal current, or any other current for that matter, around this area. Could the gearbox be broken? Or could it be…

"Oh, bugger."

I promptly pulled back on the revs until the throttle was in the up-position. As I did, the little red button on the side popped out with a merry 'click', indicating that the gearbox had yet again been engaged. I pushed the throttle from neutral into forward and could feel the boat shoot off as the propeller started churning its way through the water.

Swede, you are such an idiot.

Horrendously blonde moment number 4

So there we were, three merry men in a canoe.

Well, almost anyway. The story takes place during my YachtMaster preparation week on a day when we had actually been blown in and had to stay overnight on a floating pontoon somewhere in the River Fal between Truro and Falmouth in the UK. Since there was nothing to do on the boat, on the pontoon, in the pissing rain, the three aspiring commercial skippers that we were thought it a good idea to go to the pub and get drunk. And since we were moored on said pontoon, the dinghy had to be our method of transportation.

There are so many faults in this scenario already.

Right. So let's inflate the dinghy then. We all know how this usually goes; one poor sod is struggling away with the pump while the others stand around mocking and making comments on why it takes such a long time. In this case, the poor sod happened to be the Swede.

"I could really use that drink now."

Finally, the dinghy was inflated and pushed into the water. The 2.5 horsepower, 4-stroke outboard was fitted, and the three of us climbed aboard with the great anticipation of a cold pint in the nice, warm pub over on the other side of the river bend. Since I had worked as a tour guide for over a year driving outboard dinghies around in the Caribbean, and since I was the one to inflate the bloody thing, I took the liberty to have some fun by driving it as well. Open the air vent, choke out, pull, choke in, pull, engine start. And we were off to have the best beer of our lives.

The little engine ticked away happily, and we did surprisingly well with the three of us in the dinghy. The heavy weather was not really that noticeable where we were, and only a tiny chop hit the bow of the dinghy as we headed right into the wind. However, the rain had not stopped, and the only thing on our collective mind was to get to the pub as quickly as possible. Then the engine died.

"What the... what have you done now, Swede?" one of my friends exclaimed.

"I didn't do anything, it just died." I was as startled as the others.

"Well, get it working again!" he said as I went about to pull on the start-cord.

"Let's get the oars in the water," the apparently self-proclaimed leader said. "We'll be blown right onto the river bank if we don't do anything."

"Yup, got it," my other slightly more humble friend replied and they both started rowing with the intensity of a horse having a carrot dangling in front of its nostrils. Quite an apt comparison, come to think of it, as we could almost smell the beer being poured from the tap inside the pub. I was determined to get the outboard started and kept pulling a few times, then stopped not to flood it. I checked the air vent, but that was open and shouldn't cause a problem. The oil indicator on the side showed more than three-quarters. There was fuel inside of the tank.

"How are we doing, Swede?" demanded the wanke... skipper-to-be. "We are drifting faster than we can row, so it would be so kind of you if you can get it started any day now!"

"I don't know man," I said while shaking my head. "I've checked everything. The fuel is OK. The oil is OK. The air vent is OK. The only thing I can think of is that the sparkplugs are all wet because of the rain." I looked at the engine hoping that by some mystic psychic powers it would cough and start by itself. "I mean, I used to work with these things. For a bloody year. I should know what's wrong!" I went over the engine one more time. Check fuel in the tank. Check air vent. Check choke. Check kill-cord. Pull. Pull. Pull. Nothing happened. We had now been drifting with the wind for a good five minutes and we all started glancing nervously over towards where we started from so not to overshoot it. All of us had worked up a good sweat in our wet weather gear, my friends from rowing, and me from tinkering with the engine and jerking on the start cord. It seemed hopeless.

"Well, in that case, let's just start steering back to the training boat," the other guy said. "We're almost being blown past it."

"Just give it one more try, Swede, and then we'll go back," the first guy said.

"Ok, sure" I grabbed the cord to pull-start the engine again. Then I stopped dead in my tracks. Time seemed to slow down as everything around me appeared to go about in slow motion. The rain fell much gentler on my jacket and I could barely feel or hear the wind anymore. There was peace and serenity around me. Any moment, the cherubs would come out from behind the clouds and blow on their trumpets out of their arses.

I slowly leant forward and with my left hand I reached to the side of the engine, and flicked the fuel switch valve to 'open'.

Over a year. Over a freaking year! Working with outboards! Arrrrgggghhh!!!

Nautical terms, lesson 13

Bank

A geographic location on both land and water where a sailor will normally feel quite embarrassed to be at.

Bar

A mystical object that works as a homing beacon for a sailor, whether on land or at sea.

On Skipper Swede

During my YachtMaster training in Falmouth, I got to meet some of the wonderful and intriguing characters who have made appearances in this book. One of these characters, who I later made really good friends with, found it terribly difficult to remember the names of new people that he met, and subsequently came up with nicknames for everyone as soon as they would introduce themselves. For example, as I presented myself, he just glared at me and said:

"So, you're gonna be the Swede then."

"Ehm, but you know, that is not my name."

"Sure it is. You're the Swede."

"I'm not too sure I really like that nickname."

"Nothing wrong with The Swede, Swede."

"But...but... I was rather hoping..." I stuttered, as I secretly wanted a cool nickname like 'Captain Sparrow', 'Captain Nemo' or, by all means, 'Captain Chaos'. In comparison, I thought that 'The Swede' represented the sound a pancake makes when it accidentally flops onto the kitchen floor.

"Nah, the Swede is great, Swede," he mused and went back to the classroom. "Let's get on with the secondary port tidal calculations now, shall we!"

Bugger. That's it then, and it's gonna be stuck with me from now on, I thought helplessly.

I had no idea then how right I was, as it took only 3 days for the population of the whole marina to call me 'The Swede'. After a day of training, the bar staff at the yacht club would greet me with "Hi Swede, how was it out there today?" and not even flinch when saying it. I would overhear people as I walked into a room or from behind a corner "Have you seen Swede?" and I could swear they didn't know my birth name. Even the RYA instructors started calling me Swede, and joked that I should have the nickname on my certificates instead of my real name, as no-one in the sailing world would recognise me otherwise.

I suppose that was when I gave up on the whole thing and surrendered to the inevitability of me as 'The Swede' for the rest of my sailing life. And when I passed my exams and got my certification, I quite naturally received the title of Skipper, hence 'Skipper Swede'.

My friend who came up with the nickname is also someone who is quick on taking the piss, who loves a good wind-up, and who can't resist a good joke. So whenever someone new and uninitiated came along, they would as a rule inquire: "Who is the Swede?" My friend would proceed by doing a fantastic impersonation of Jeremy Clarkson, and any fan of Top Gear will clearly see what is coming here:

"Some say he sleeps at the top of the mast, and that he has a terrible fear of heights"
"Some say he loves cats, and that he thinks the food in china is delicious"
"Some say that he once invited a parrot to his cabin and didn't come out for a month"
"Some say that he has an irrational fear of floating docks"
"Some say he sobs uncontrollably when it's dead calm"
"Some say he doesn't understand the meaning of the word 'sober'"
"Some say he has taken a vow of silence against people wearing deck shoes"
"Some say he is a real people's person, especially when he's by himself"

"All we know is, he's called the Swede!"

On money

This book is clearly an attempt to make money. Skipper Swede does not try to make a song and dance about this quite obvious fact. The reason is that owning a boat is, as the saying goes, like throwing money into the ocean. And even sailors who themselves do not own a boat, usually find themselves broke and in urgent need to find any kind of work to put food on the table, pay the astronomical bar tab, and to cry on the shoulder of the lovely ladies in the nearest brothel.

So naturally Skipper Swede, being a sailor, is also broke. And quite frankly, Skipper Swede would be very pleased if you, dear reader, would care to buy plenty more copies of this book. How about buying some for your fellow sailors, as a nice gift that will enrich their lives immensely. Perhaps you could buy 50 or so and distribute in your local Yacht Club to show what a good sport you are. Or you could get a substantial stock for your boat, as you never know when you might be running out of loo-rolls at sea.

Skipper Swede appreciates any copy purchased, and promises to spend the additional revenue on highly important and altruistic things that may make the world a better place.

Skipper Swede is also a sailor, and sailors have a nasty tendency to exaggerate, so the money will most likely be spent on booze and women instead. At least it will make Skipper Swede's world a better place.

Thank you for your contribution!

Yes, I was in fact just taking the piss...
Enjoy the index.

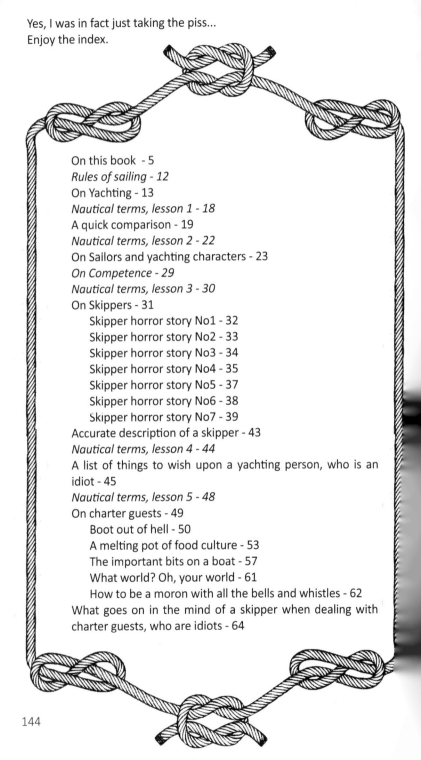

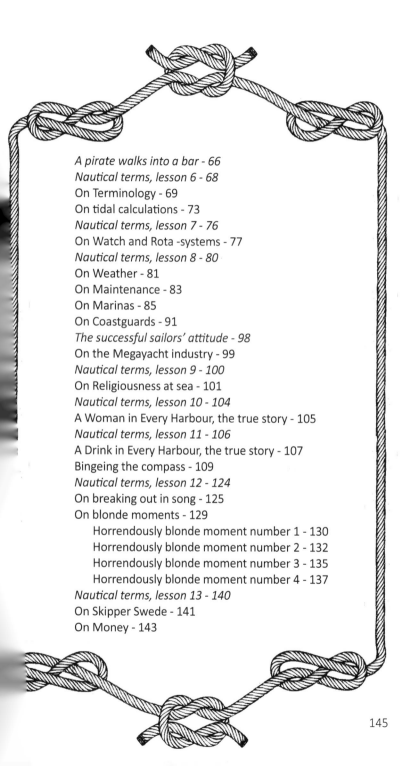

CONNECT WITH SKIPPER SWEDE

Follow on FaceBook
facebook.com/SkipperSwede

Visit the website
SkipperSwede.com

Check out the fun stuff on the website:
t-shirts, mugs, bags with pictures and quotes from the book!

Look out for the upcoming
"Skipper Swede's Little Book of Yachting - VOLUME2"
May, or may not, contain the following (and more. Maybe)

- On Crew
- On Charter Companies
- On RYA
- On Instructing
- On Marine life & Pollution
- ...and a whole bunch of new stories (courtesy of all the idiots, wankers and imbeciles I've crossed paths with recently)

Yours obnoxiously, Skipper Swede

33248488R00081

Printed in Great Britain
by Amazon